THE STAGEA SPECIAL
JAPAN DRIVEN

VOL. 1 NO.1 AUGUST 2020 — EXCLUSIVE CANADIAN STAGEA OWNERS ISSUE

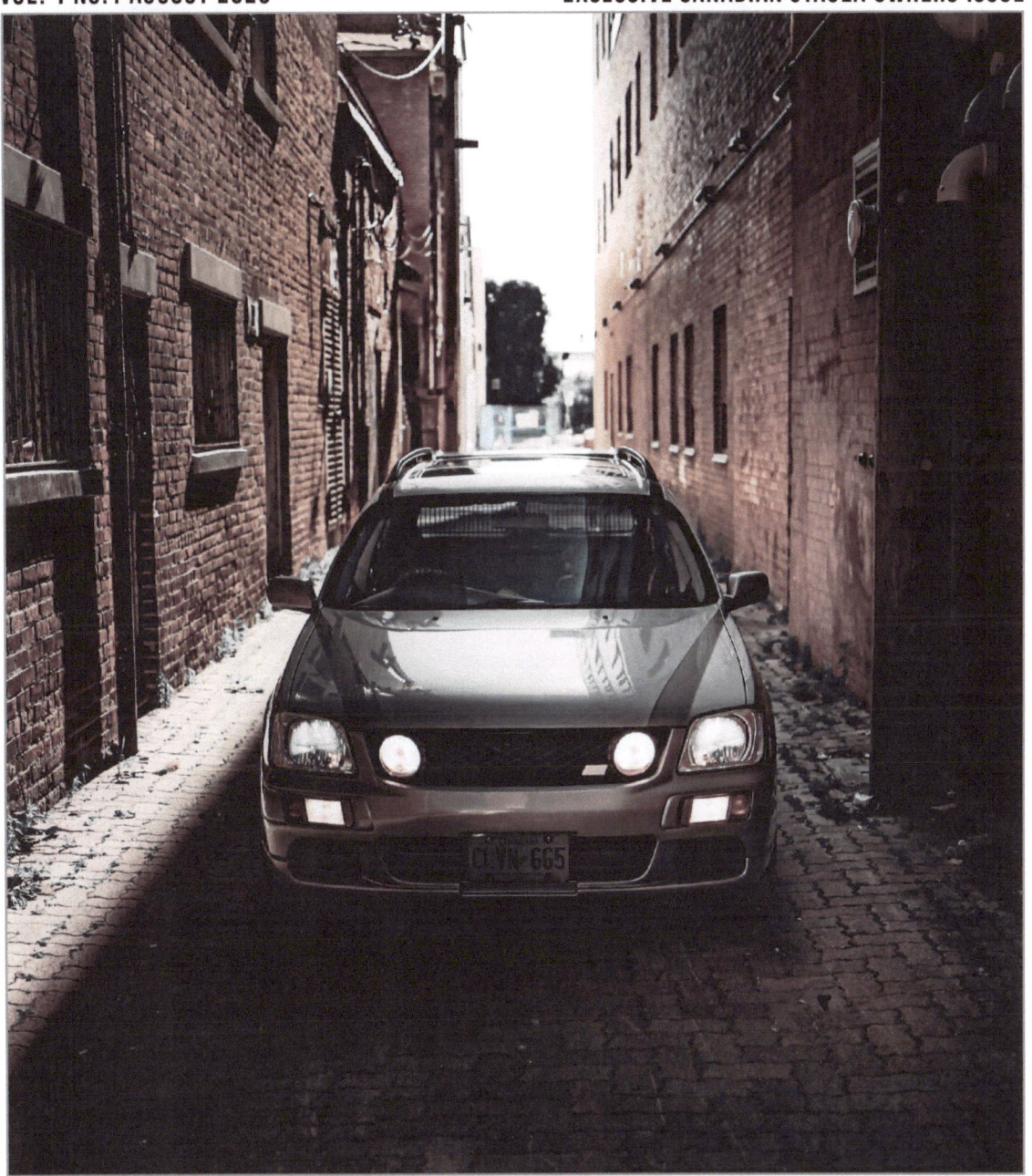

A GOD, AN ALPHA PREDATOR, GODZILLA | THE IDEAL DAILY DRIVER | AND MORE STAGEA FEATURES

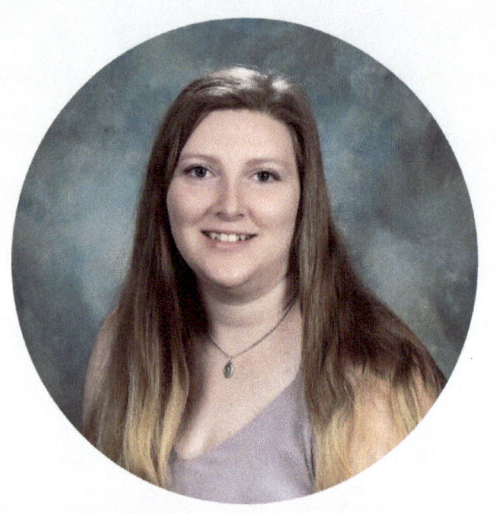

EDITOR'S NOTE

Hey there! For those who don't already know me, my name is Kaitlyn Kjargaard. I reside in Regina, Saskatchewan, Canada with my boyfriend, Samuel Gee, and our dog, Mushu. Currently we own a 1999 Nissan Stagea RS4V and just added a 2001 Mitsubishi Evolution VII to our small collection last December. The amount of help with this project was overwhelming, but in a good way! I had been wanting to start up a magazine for quite some time now. When I found out that I had to create my very own magazine from scratch for a graphic design assignment, I knew it was a great opportunity to get started. I'd like to thank our fellow members from the Canadian Stagea Owners Facebook group for the immense amount of support and help with sharing their stories and the great memories that have come with our time of enjoying these unique yet beautiful vehicles. You will not meet a more helpful, kind, and supportive group than that of a Stagea owner. Enjoy the very first issue of Japan Driven, and future issues that are yet to come!

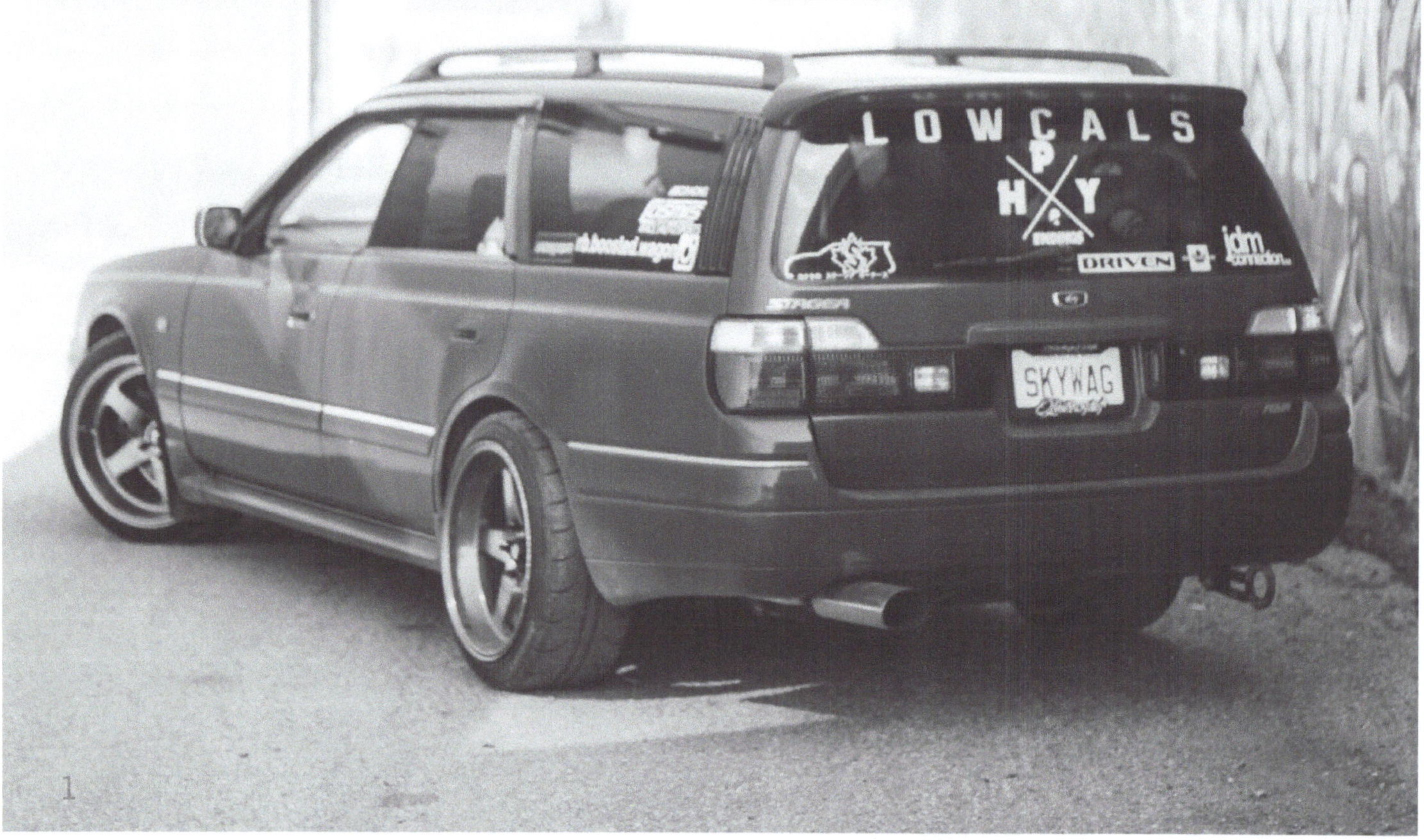

CONTENTS

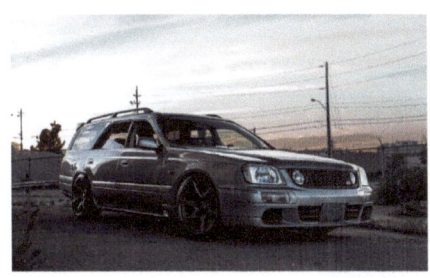

PAGES 3-4 — Not Just A Pretty Face
Douglas's 1999 Nissan Stagea RS4

PAGES 5-6 — A God, An Alpha Predator, Godzilla
Devin's 1999 Nissan Stagea RSV

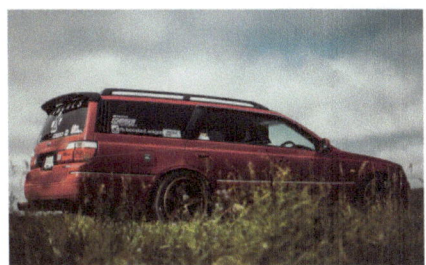

PAGES 7-8 — The Ideal Daily Driver
Coen's 2000 Stagea RS4V – DayZ Edition

PAGES 9-12 — It's That Kind Of Thrill
Sammy's 1999 Stagea RS4V

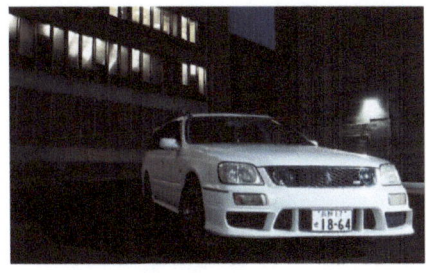

PAGES 13-14 — Clean, Sleek, & Innovative
Liam's 1999 Stagea RS4S – DayZ Edition

PAGES 15-16 — Seeing Double? Us Too!
Josh's 1999 Nissan Stagea RS4S

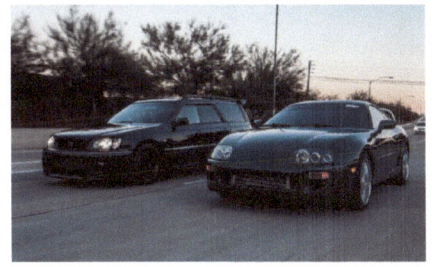

PAGES 17-18 — Fueled For That Driven Life
James's 1998 Nissan Stagea 260RS Autech

PAGES 19-20 — Clean Slate
Joel's 2001 Nissan Stagea NM35 250T RX4

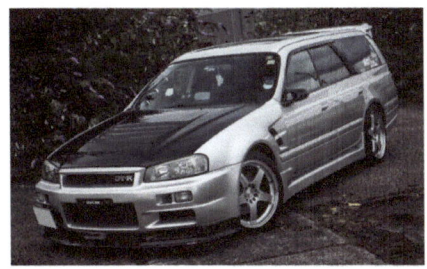

PAGES 21-22 — New Class
Jonathan's 1997 Nissan Stagea RS4

Not Just A

Douglas, 28

@jdm.douglas
Ontario, Canada
1999 Nissan Stagea RS4

Running an RB25DET engine, BC Racing extreme lows, Kansei Tandem wheels wrapped in Firehawk Indy 500s, HKS Racing blow-off valve, cat-back exhaust with blast pipe, and a Greddy air intake.

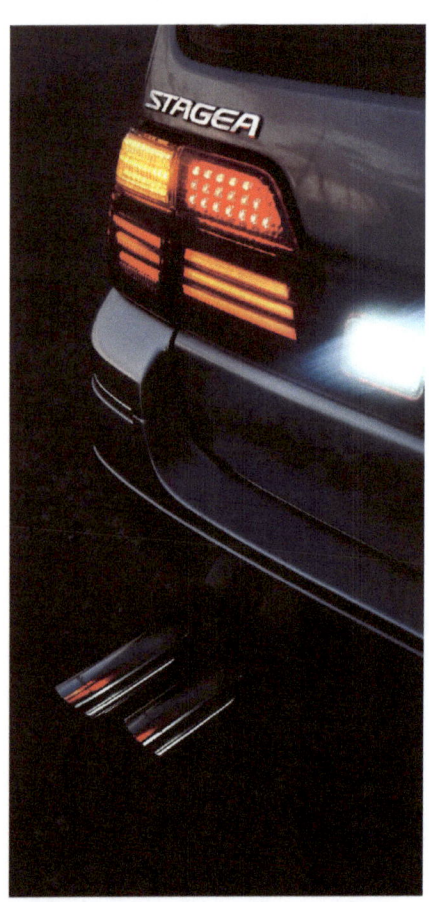
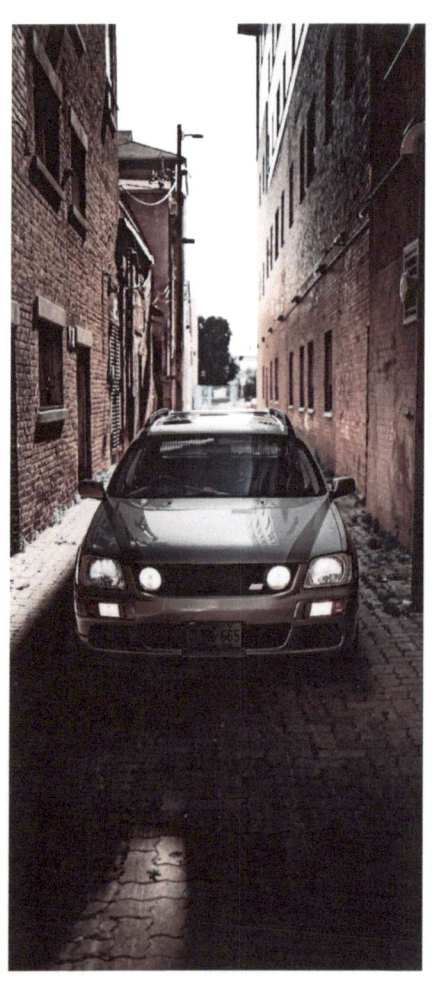
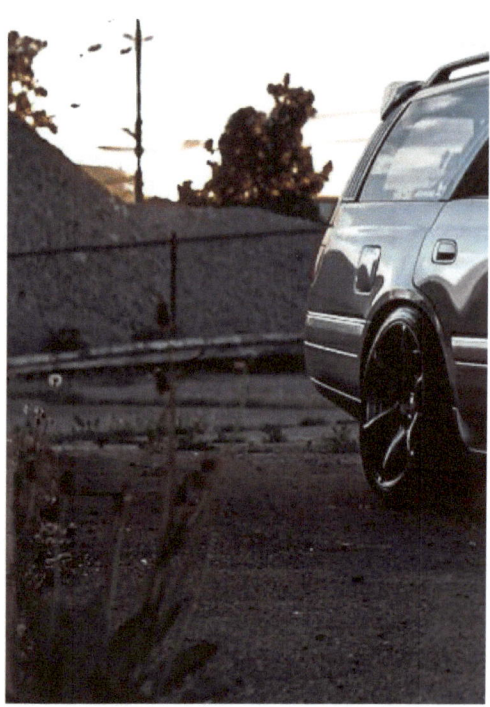

Pretty Face

ステージア

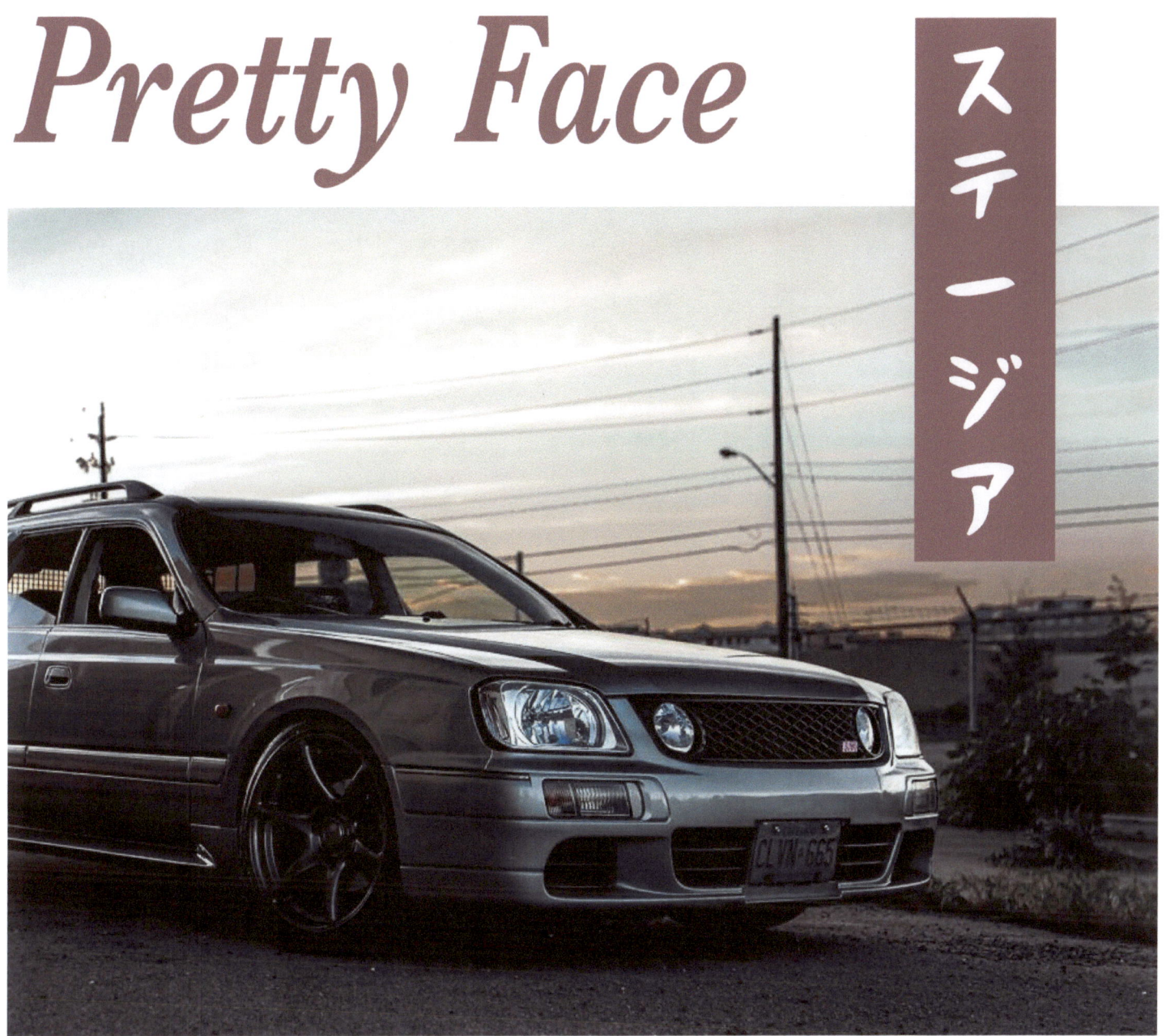

Douglas bought his 1999 Nissan Stagea RS Four about a year ago, and had it shipped from Alberta to his home in Ontario. Before his dad passed in a car accident, his dad had a Toyota Celica and that's when Douglas found his passion for cars. "I wanna say it's in my blood, but I found the car scene at a really low point in my life and it brought me some happiness, so I stuck with it", recounted Douglas. He plans to continue his project by swapping out the front end with an R34 with tons of carbon fiber bits, eventually some new wheels, and possibly a colour change with air ride suspension. Douglas recalled his favorite memory of his car, "Picking her up, still a surreal day. The drive there and home to get her from being shipped in."

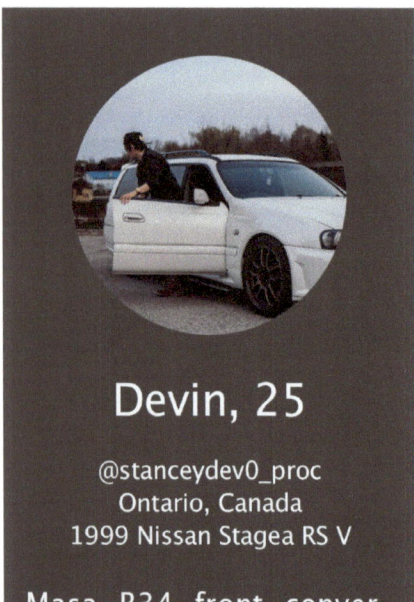

Devin, 25

@stanceydev0_proc
Ontario, Canada
1999 Nissan Stagea RS V

Masa R34 front conversion with genuine Nissan bumper/lip, Works CR Kai 18x9.5 wheels, aftermarket HID setup, custom polyurethane side splitters and canards, Nardi steering wheel on a NRG quick release, carbon shift knob with shift boot, custom paddle shifters, Blitz boost and power meter gauges and full led interior lighting, RB25det NEO, stock turbo with aftermarket steel compressor, Nistune ecu, Blitz boost controller, Blitz power meter, Greddy front mount intercooler, Trust intake pod filter, Greddy spark plugs (0.8 gapped), Splitfire coil packs, Tomei headgasket, Kakimoto titanium exhaust from down pipe back, Apexi exhaust valve, Billet differential mounts, Cusco coilovers, Cusco toe arms, 300 ZX TT rear brake conversion on Stoptech Rotors and Brembo pads.

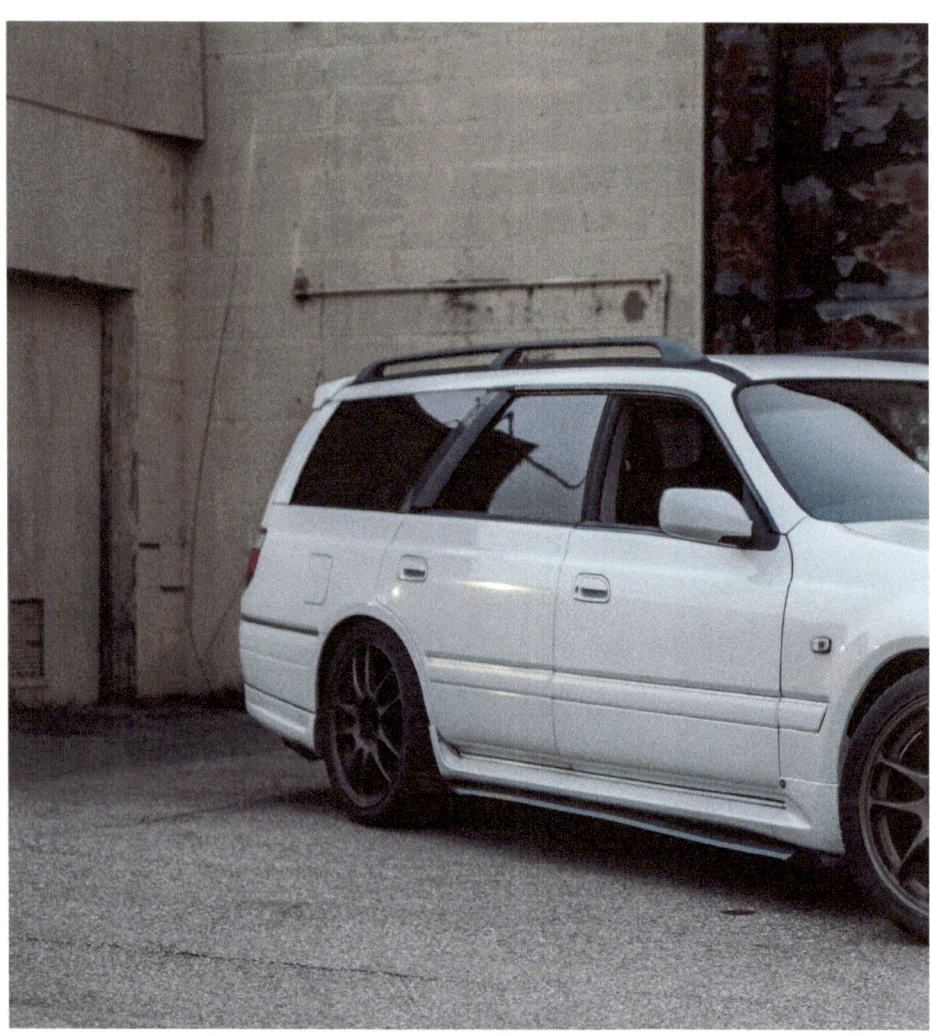

A GOD, AN ALPHA PREDATOR
GODZILLA

Devin has had his 1999 Nissan Stagea RS V for nine months now. He imported it in December of 2019. "I've been into cars my whole life since a small kid. My mom's side of the family are mechanics and bodywork guys, and in general into cars. My dad raised me into mechanics. I started with dirt bikes and working on them before I started buying cars at around age 15." Devin reminisces. "I've always liked the body lines and look of a Stagea personally. Being a Laurel/Skyline base, it had the cool factor of a Skyline, but the practicality of a wagon. Every kid growing up on the old Fast & Furious movies wanted a Skyline R34, but couldn't afford one once we were old enough. I already had five cars in my possession by age 24. I didn't need another coupe, but a Stagea was a perfect excuse to get an import. It just made

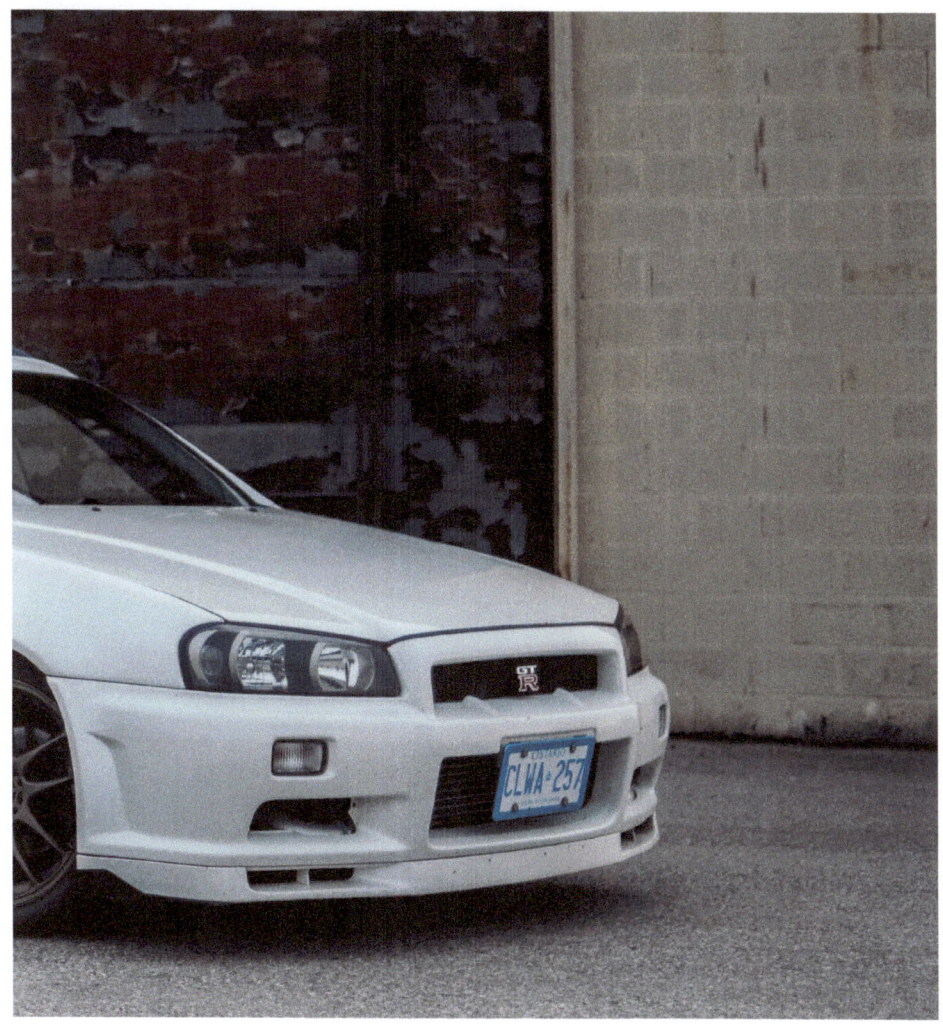
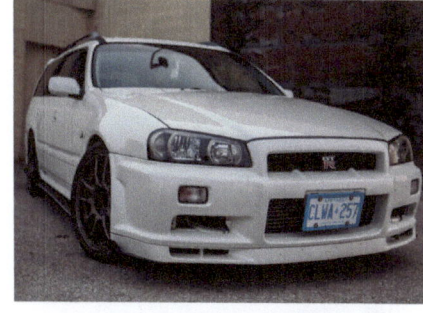
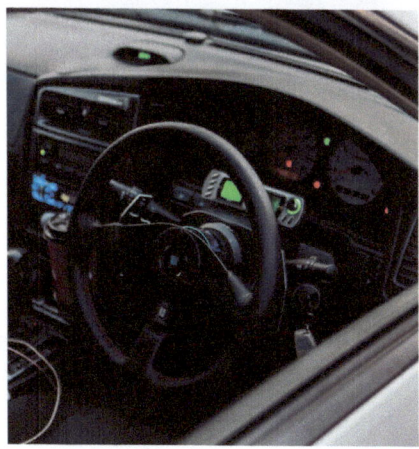
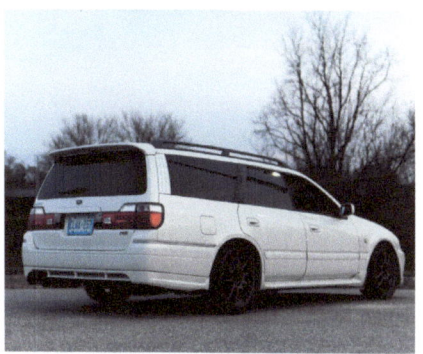
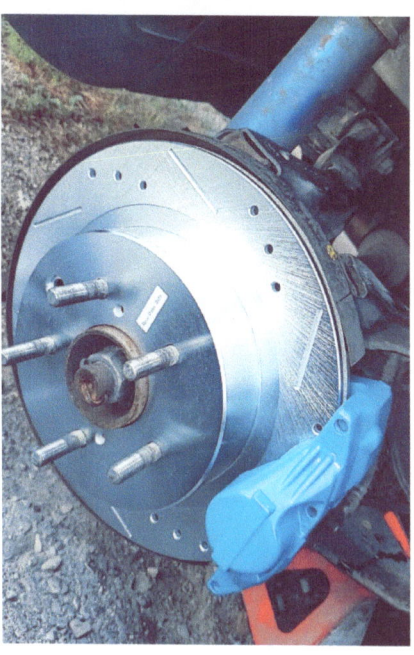

sense. I can tow my drift car or motocross bikes with it, boost around daily, and reliably enjoying the RB under the hood while modifying it. It really is a practical Skyline in my head, and putting the R34 front conversion on made it just that!" Devin states that he plans to get 350z Brembo four-pot front brakes, a custom hitch to tow his AE86 drift car and a full respray. "I plan on getting track days in with it and going to as many meets and shows and just getting enjoyment out of the car!" When asked what his favorite memory was with the car he commented, "It's hard to pick a single memory, but taking my girlfriend out in it on our first experience with a rhd car and driving one will always be pretty priceless! Other than that, the first cruise with a good friend of mine in his Miata and fist-pounding each others fists on the highway was pretty cool!" Devin wanted to add, "The Stagea community in Canada is growing and I'm very happy to see that! These rwd RS models do not have much of a following themselves or info on modifying them. I do wish to help the community of owners by documenting my car as I work/build on it to further part accessibility for the owners."

The Ideal Daily Driver

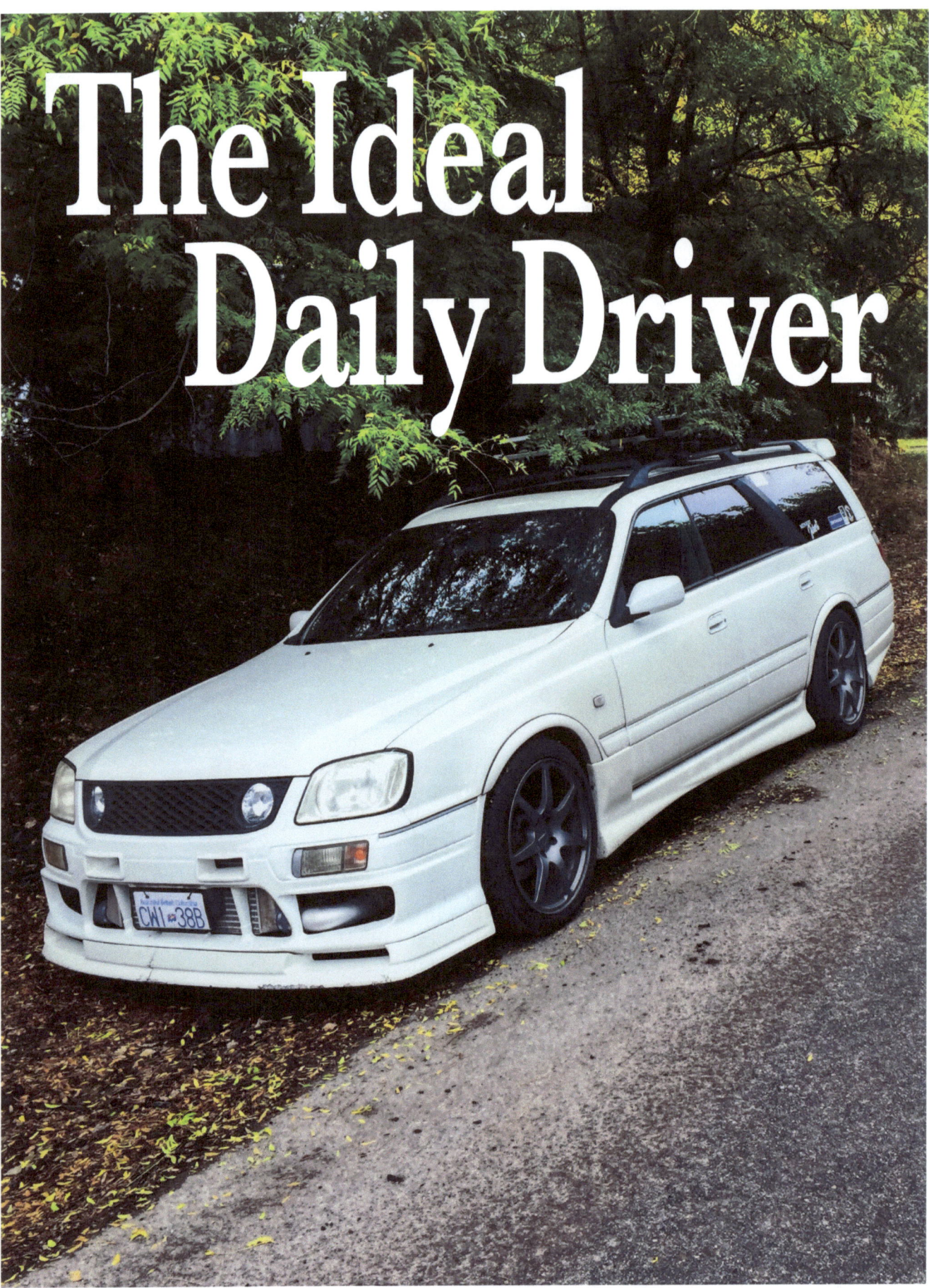

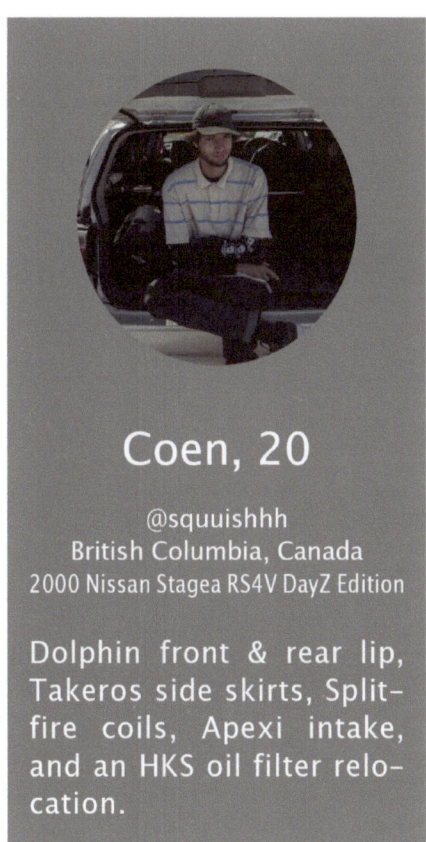

Coen, 20

@squuishhh
British Columbia, Canada
2000 Nissan Stagea RS4V DayZ Edition

Dolphin front & rear lip, Takeros side skirts, Splitfire coils, Apexi intake, and an HKS oil filter relocation.

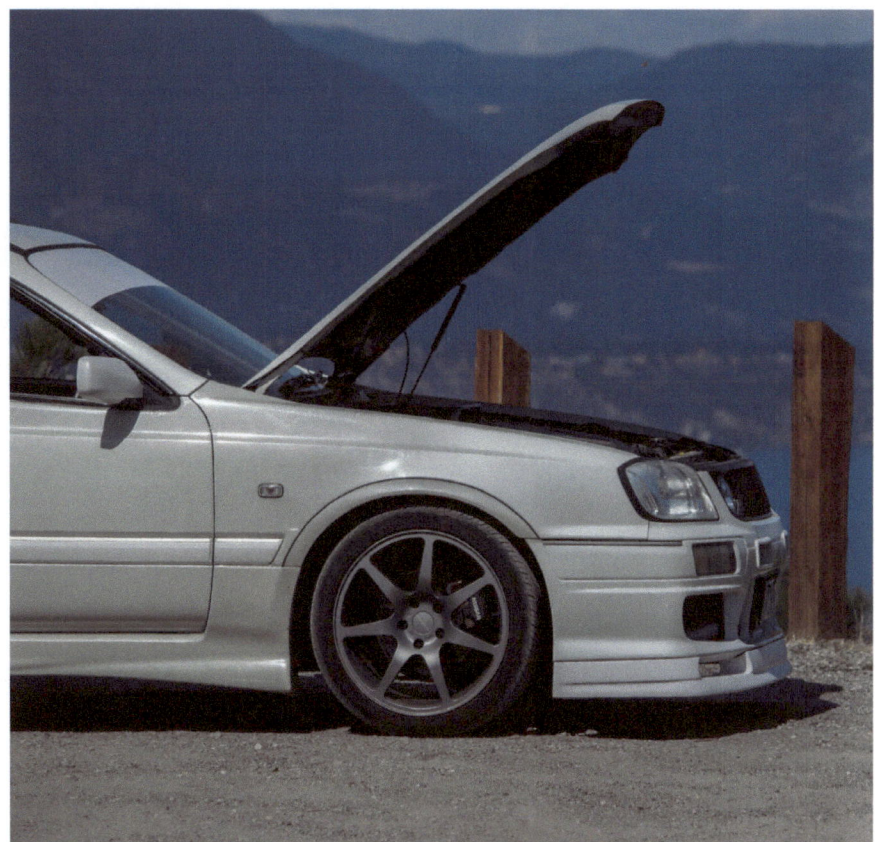

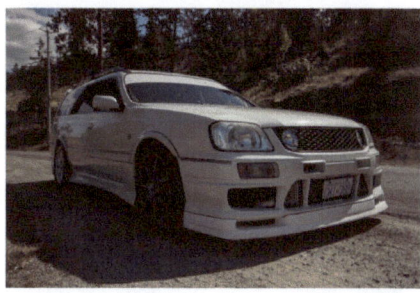

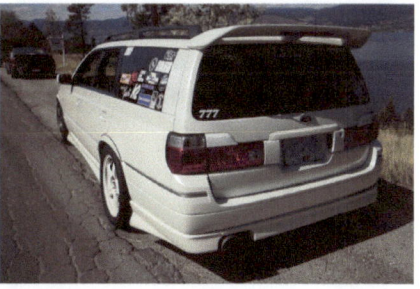

"I've owned it for 4 years now, as I bought it when I was in grade 12. I imported it myself with the help of some of my friends in Japan. My dad was a car guy, always building classic cars and going to car shows all over North America, driving the cars he built. This got me into cars and it's been downhill from there. When I was younger my dad built my mom a 1964 Bel Air wagon and I've always had a soft spot for wagons since then. Previously before owning the Stagea, I had 2 Skylines, but always looked at Stageas and thought they were amazing looking cars. The practicality of having a wagon was also a plus for me, even though I don't use the trunk much. I imported it because it was exactly what I was looking for body-wise. It's a daily so I haven't done much to building it, but I've installed Splitfire coils, an Apexi intake to get rid of the HKS mushroom filter, and an HKS oil filter relocation. My future goals for it is to keep it as clean as possible as well as manual swap it; I have all the parts, I have just been lazy with the swap. I also plan on doing some small horsepower gains eventually, but even after 4 years, I find it still has plenty of power for me and I find it very fun. My favorite memory is driving it down to Nissanfest in Monroe, Washington and having the border guard talk to me about the car for 30 minutes while there was a huge lineup behind me."

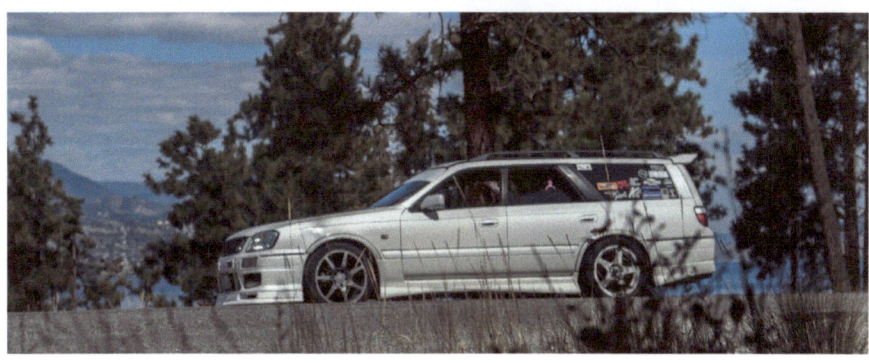

It's That Kind

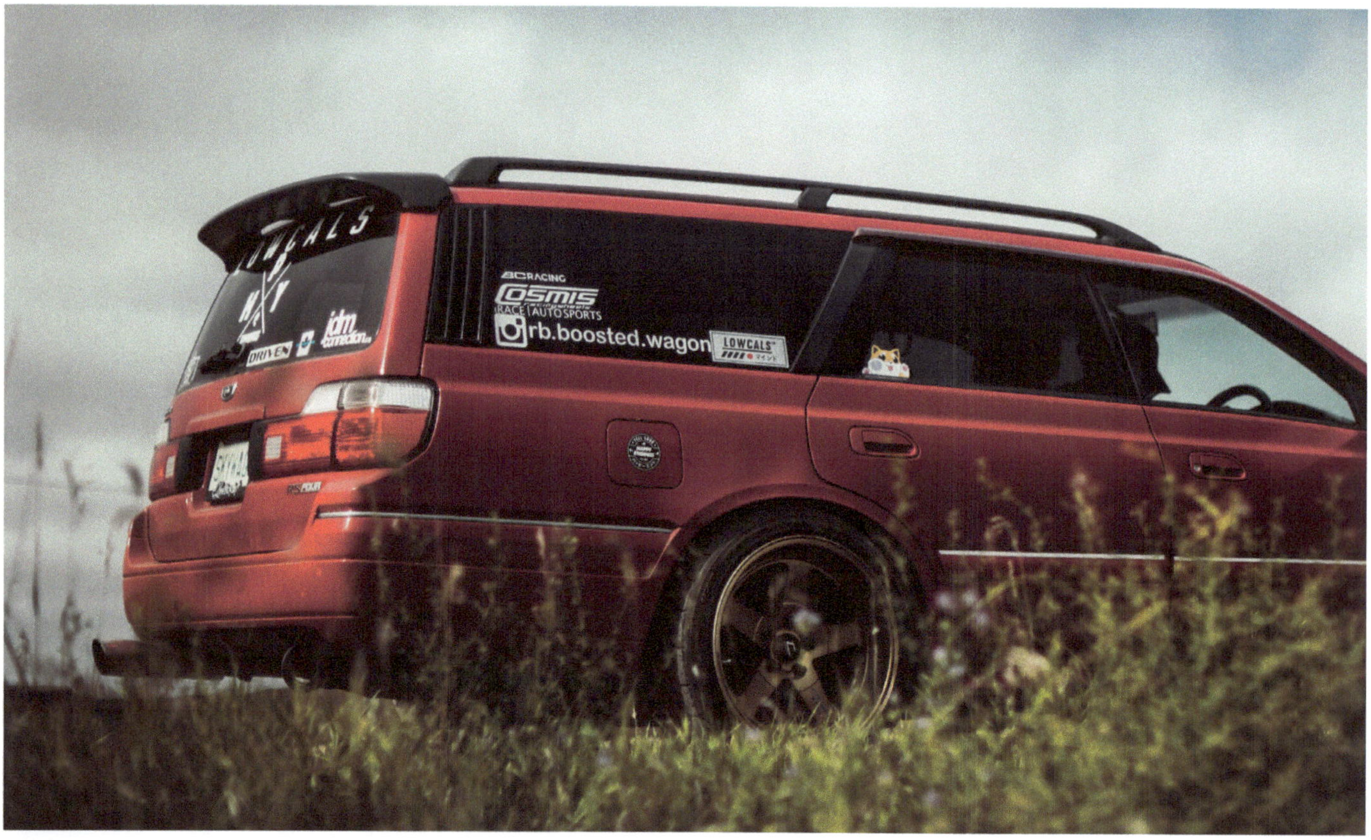

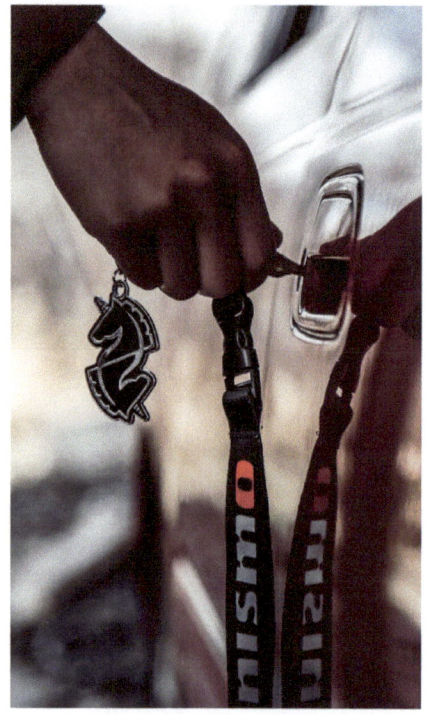

"I've had my stagea for a little over 2 and a half years, but plated for about 2 years, as it took quite a while to get parts to pass it's provincial safety.

When I first decided to actually go through with buying my Stagea, I began looking locally, well more so one located already in Canada. The reason for this was that I figured that they would be better looked after than straight from Japan. My ideal Stagea that I was looking for was a series 2 RS Four S, but at that time, there were maybe 2 that matched what I was wanting and around the $10,000 mark. Money was tight, so I decided to check out the series 2 RS Four models, which were about half the price of the manuals. There were only series 1 Stageas posted, which I wasn't too fond of the front. With car season quickly approaching, I finally decided to pull the plug on buying local. I messaged William at JDM Connections, who imports vehicles for a living, about importing an automatic Stagea from Japan. I was getting desperate, and after working with William and passing on a bunch of Stageas due to rust, corrosion, and engine problems, we finally found the right Stagea. There was also a small bonus that I was excited about; it was bright, bold, red instead of the generic black or white. We put our bid in and ended up winning it for lower than my budget. He made

Of Thrill

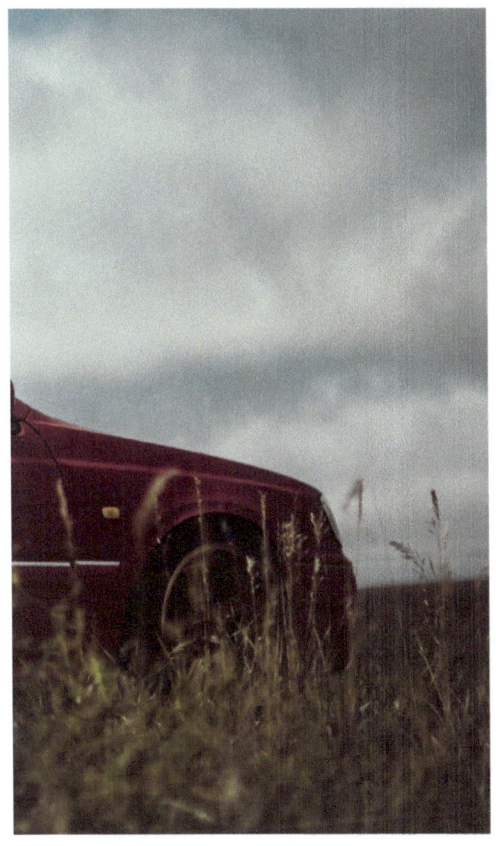

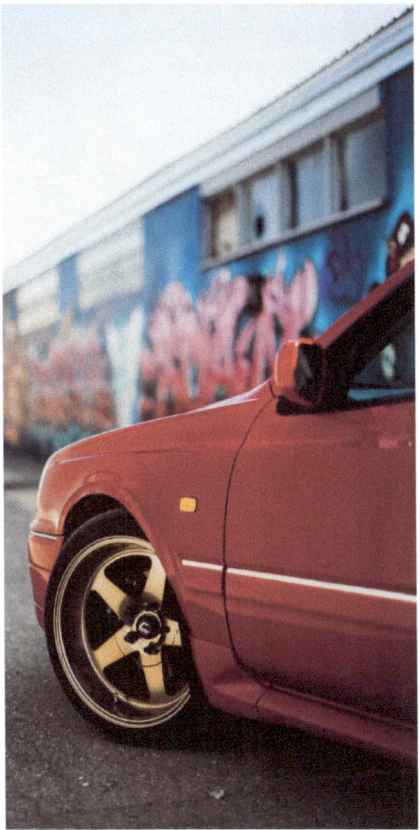

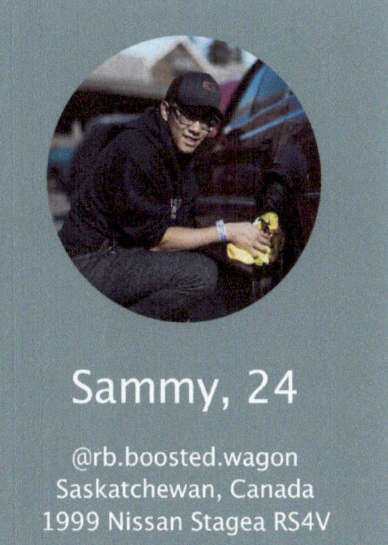

Sammy, 24

@rb.boosted.wagon
Saskatchewan, Canada
1999 Nissan Stagea RS4V

18"x10"+20 Cosmis Racing XT005R wheels in hyper bronze finish, Silver's Neomax Coilovers, straight-piped exhaust, Pioneer double-din stereo with a JL Audio 10" subwoofer, custom-made Stagea tsurikawas and mirror hanger, Greddy Type-FV blow-off valve, Blitz cone filter, Mishimoto aluminum radiator, ISR Performance silicone rad hoses, Works Bell short hub with an NRG version-3 quick release and a limited edition 1 of 250 that will ever be made Nardi and Vertex collaboration deep dish 340mm steering wheel, and full led upgrade.

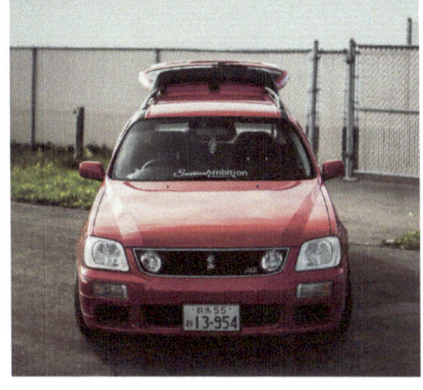

sure it was mechanically sound, and so the waiting game began for when it arrived in Canada.

When I was little, my dad owned an old 90's BMW E36. He was part of the local BMW Club and would always bring me to the meets. My uncle also worked and still works at the bmw dealership. My dad also took me to see The Fast and the Furious: Tokyo Drift at a local theatre. This marked the moment where I became interested in cars with a slight bias towards imports. Years went by and I quickly became addicted to the whole Fast and Furious series, getting more and more interested in imports. Growing up, I was bullied in elementary school all the way through high school. Because of this, I never really had any friends. Most of the time, I kept to myself, but when I was in high school, I tried finding friends. With no luck, I ended up going clique to clique, from robotics club, to jocks, to the preppy groups, and all the way to the smokers and druggies. After bad experiences with the last clique, I somehow ended up hanging out with the Philipino students as they were very inviting and accepting. I discovered a lot of them drove lowered/slammed Honda Civics and due to me being into imports, low and behold, we clicked. We all became friends till it was time to graduate, and slowly we all parted

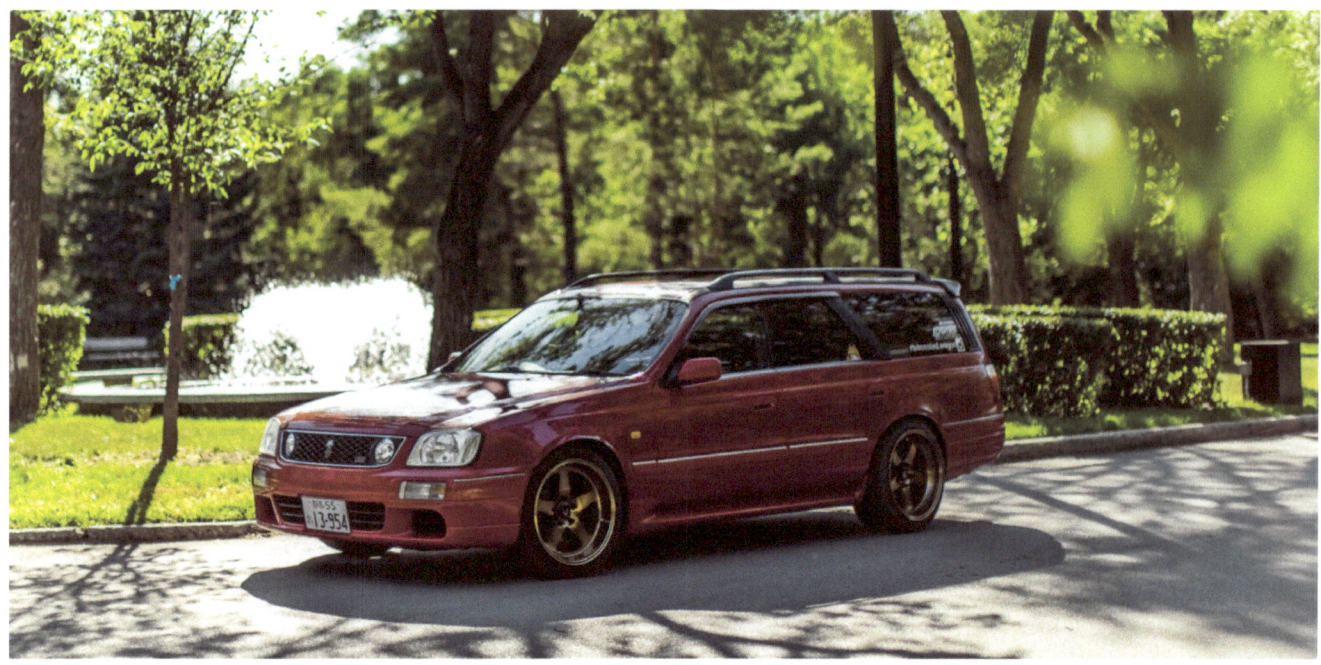

ways. I just owned a 2003 BMW E46 and never really got to do anything to it, other than wheels and a sound system. High school also marked the time where I was introduced to the whole importing from Japan option. Every week it seemed as though I'd be browsing the auction lists as well as what they already had in stock in Edmonton.

While browsing the auction sites in high school, I stumbled upon the Nissan Stageas. I found one that became my dream car. It was manual, unique, and looked aggressive AF. (I just recently found out that a friend of mine in the Stagea community actually purchased that exact Stagea I idolized in high school). I knew at this point I could never afford it, but one can also dream. As time passed, I forgot about the Stagea and importing from Japan, but still stayed very active in the car community. Years later in life, I met my wonderful girlfriend who was also into cars. We finally decided together that we would budget and find me a cool car since my old car got totaled and I was driving a leased Toyota Corolla. We both loved the idea of importing a car once I introduced her to the idea of getting a car from Japan. I wanted something cool, unique, something that is very uncommon, and a head turner. We also discussed the idea of starting a family and being smarter and more mature, so something that also had 4 doors and space for hauling stuff. I stumbled on the Stagea again and my love and dreams sparked. I was torn between the Nissan Stagea and the Mitsubishi Legnum, both were cool, aggressive, right-hand-drive station wagons. After plenty of research, I decided on the Stagea. Why you may ask? I've wanted a skyline ever since seeing the Fast and the Furious series, and saw the Stagea Shares the same engine as the Nissan Skyline R34. I fell in love and soon my dream became a reality.

As for future plans, I don't really have much planned other than some aesthetics as it is my daily driver and I want it to still stay reliable. I also plan on getting rid of it to get a manual Stagea to build further. I'd like to either paint or vinyl wrap the car a candy apple red or similar and switch to an HKS Super Sequential Version 4 blow-off valve.

My favorite memory would be taking the Stagea with my girlfriend and I for a snowboard trip in Manitoba and spending quality time together."

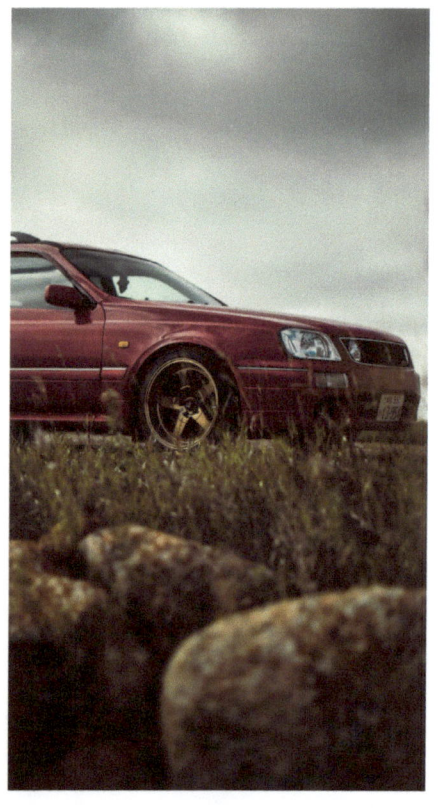

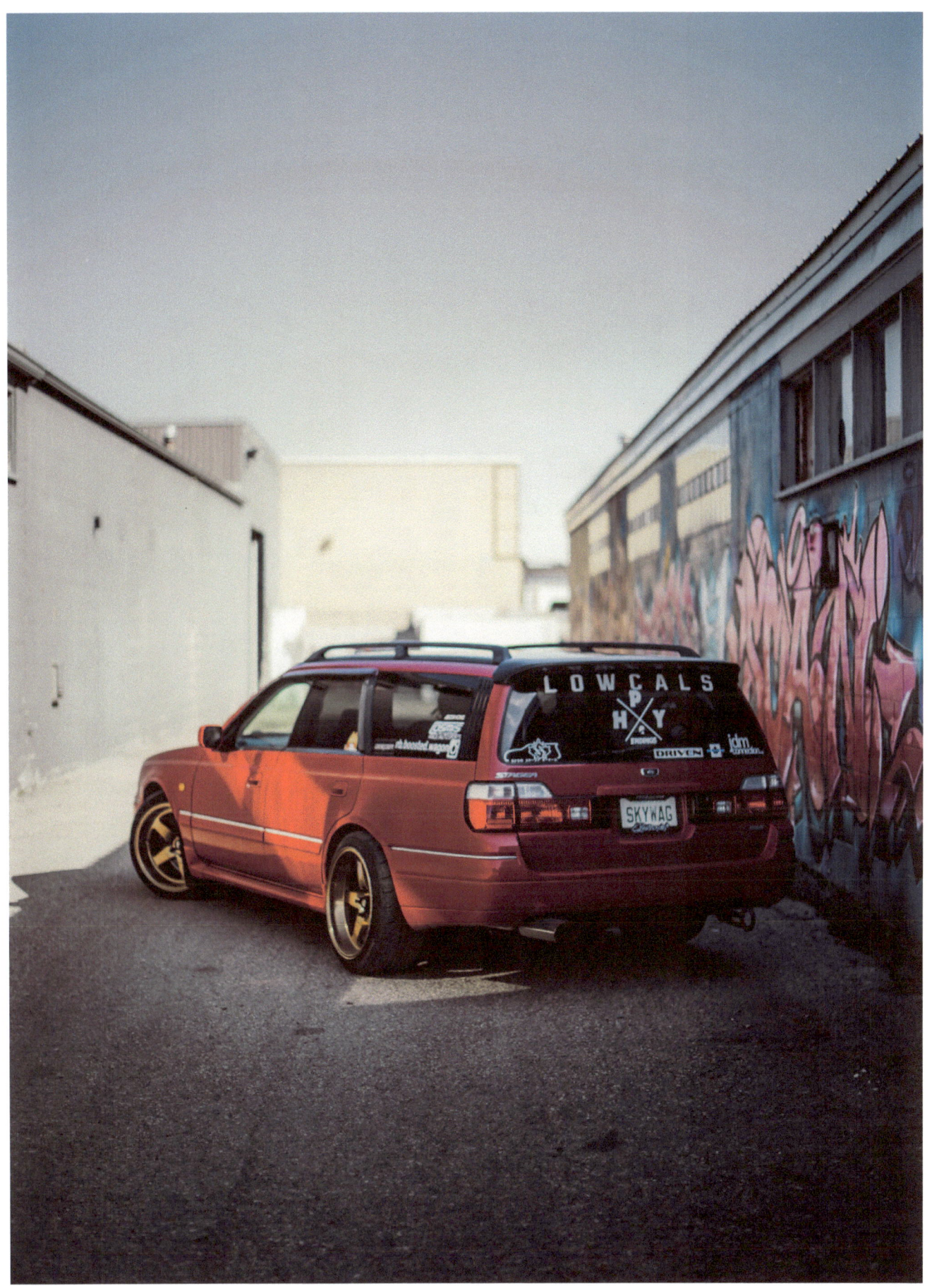

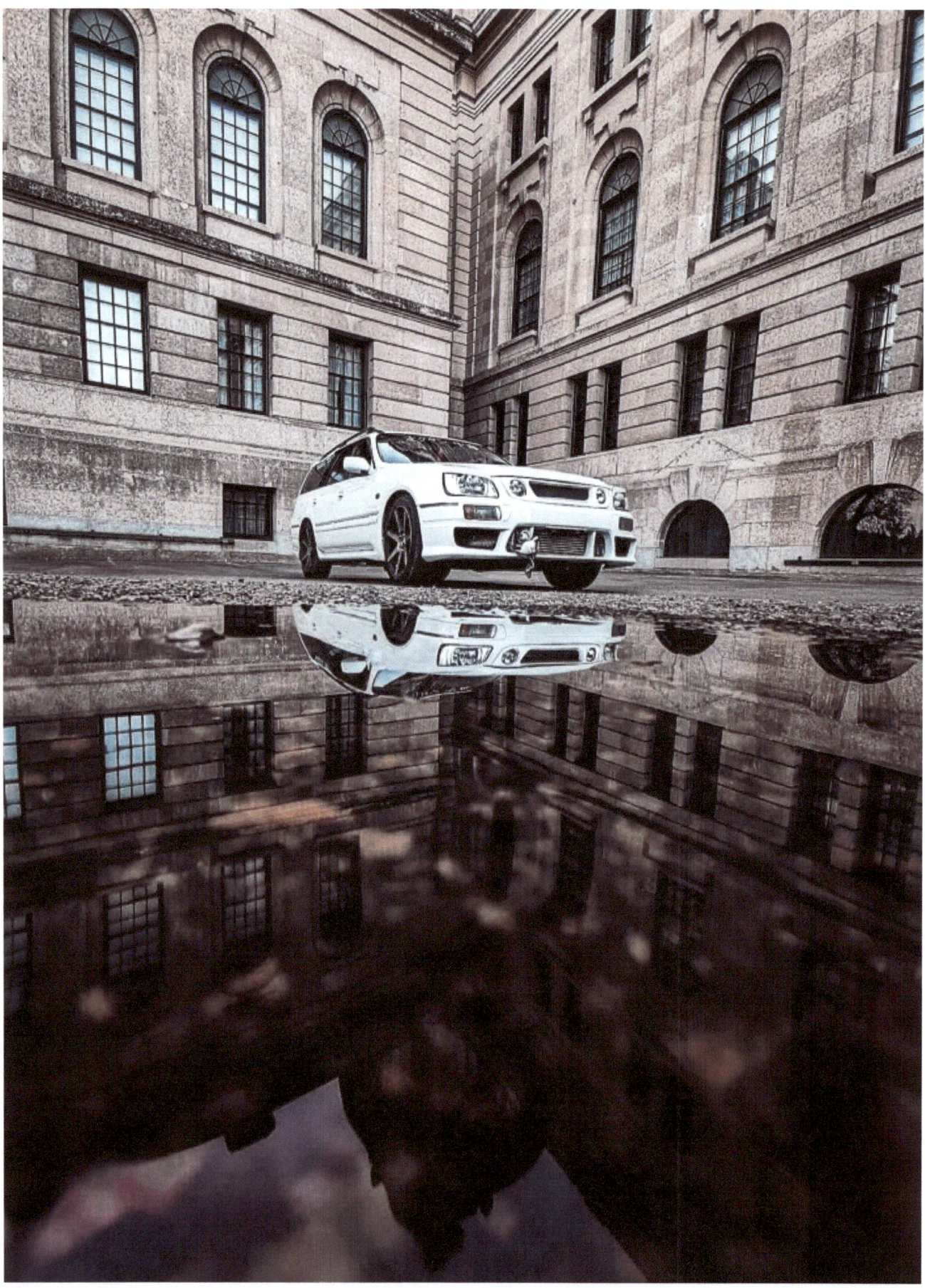

Clean, Sleek, & Innovative

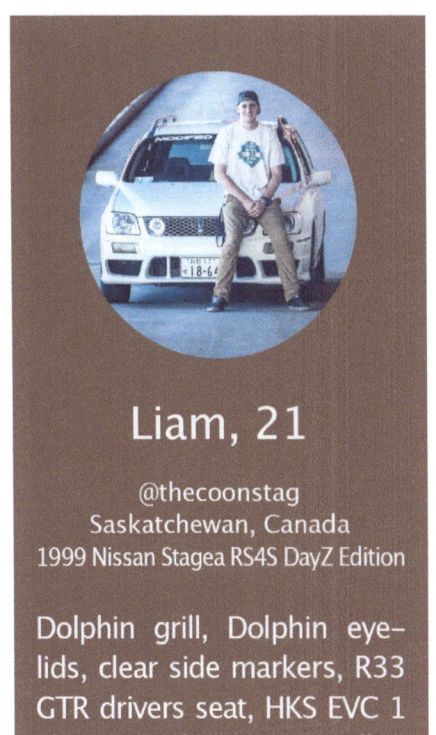

Liam, 21

@thecoonstag
Saskatchewan, Canada
1999 Nissan Stagea RS4S DayZ Edition

Dolphin grill, Dolphin eyelids, clear side markers, R33 GTR drivers seat, HKS EVC 1 electronic boost controller, Bee-r rev limiter, Crown Royal shift boot, Glowshift triple pillar pod gauges (boost, AF/R, oil pressure), BC Racing coilovers, Hicas delete, Niche M150 Verona wheels, drilled and slotted rotors, Blitz oversized front mount intercooler, Greddy type S blow off valve, high flow turbo, Autobahn 88 downpipe with screamer, Apexi intake, and a 3 inch straight pipe.

Liam has had his 1999 Nissan Stagea RS4S Dayz Edition for four years now. He had traded his Forester for it locally. "My whole family was into cars since my grandpa, and I guess you could say it was passed down, it all started with a 1997 BMW 320i. The bigger factor of choosing the Stagea is that it's a wagon and I have a thing for wagons. Coming in second would be the fact that it's an RB so lots of parts and easy to work on. I have done a lot of maintenance work such as: timing belt, water pump, changing front half shafts multiple times, windshield and few other maintenance items. Future goal which was supposed to be achieved next winter but buying a house got in the way, 450whp(was going to get it built at boost factory) Tomei 265 degrees cams, rebuild turbo, full rebuild on motor, Greddy front facing plenum, 1000cc injectors, G35 throttle body, link g4+ ecu, Bosch 088 fuel pump, and Audi R8 coil packs. Hopefully this winter I will also get my R33 GTR calipers on as well. My favorite memory was driving to Driven in Calgary and cruising in the mountains. It really felt truly perfect with the Stagea. I would recommend a Stagea to a lot of people since parts are available almost anywhere and it's a wagon so insurance is cheaper than R34 GTT. You basically have a R34 GTT with half the price and cheaper insurance, but you still get the looks from everyone. I've met a lot of people through Stageas and they are by far the most accepting people and they never turn you down when you ask for help even if it's for something very basic!"

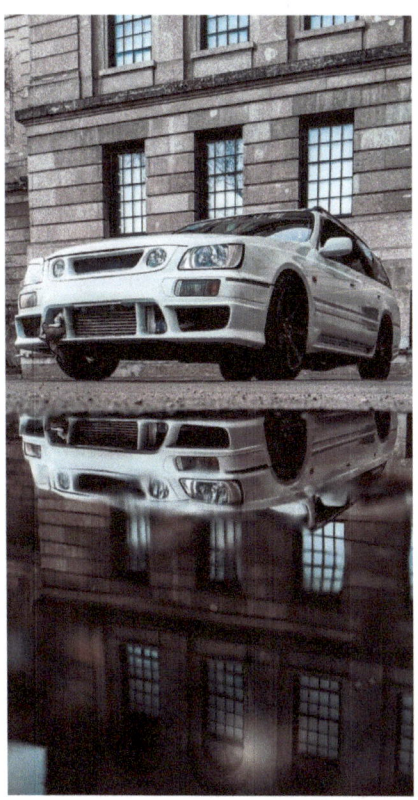

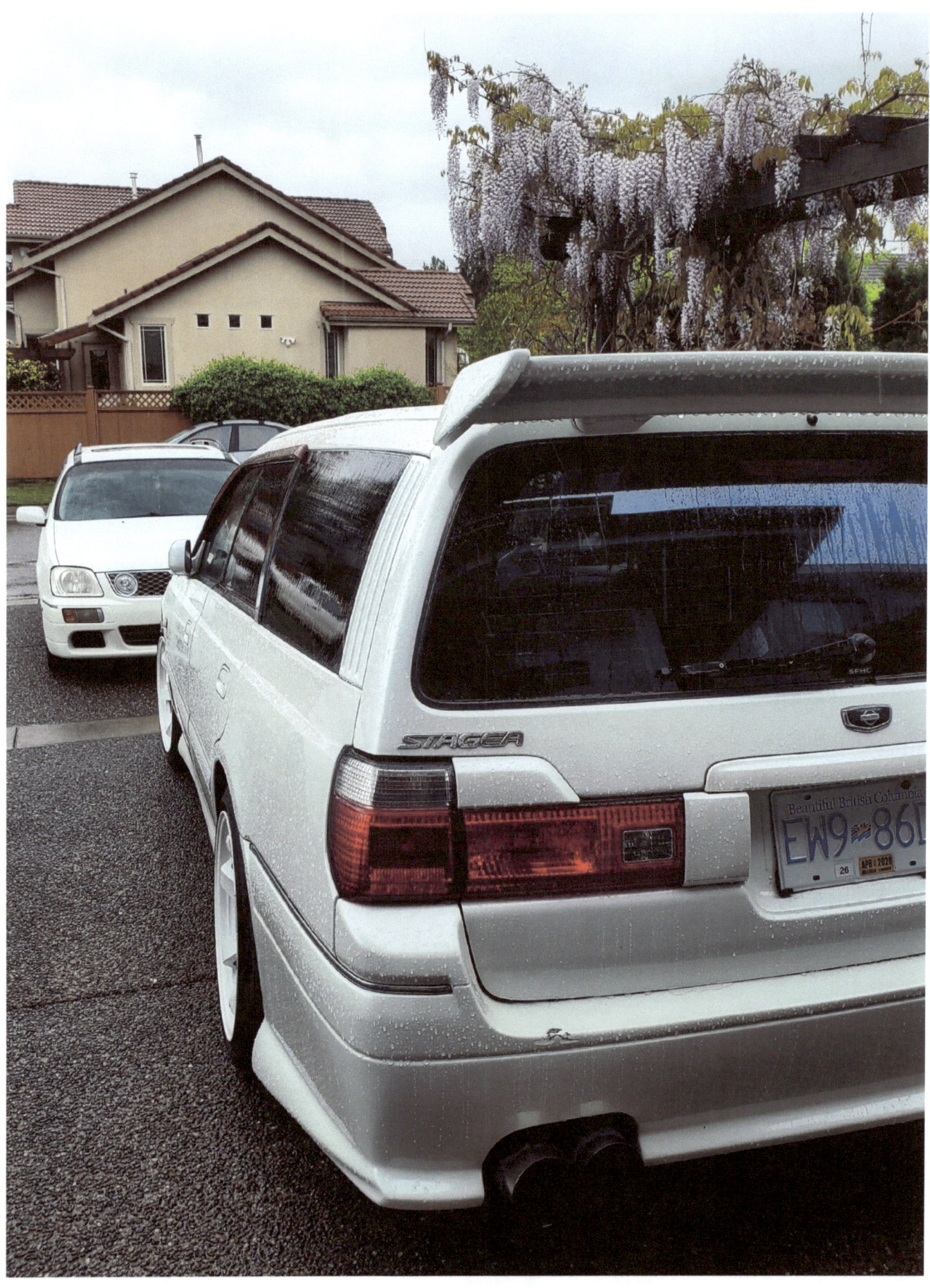

Seeing Double? Us Too!

Josh, 33

British Columbia, Canada
1999 Nissan Stagea RS4S

HPI FMIC coilovers, turbo back 3" exhaust, ECU master EMU black standalone unit, wideband kit, flex fuel kit to run E85, PHP boost control kit, Deatschwerks 1000cc injectors & a DW400 fuel pump, Spectrum Motorsports hi-flow replacement turbo, Audi A4 coilpack conversion, Performance World BOV, and Avid 18x9 wrapped with 255/50ZR18 gforce comp 2.

In May of 2020, Josh locally purchased a 1999 Nissan Stagea RS4S after having owned an RS4 for two years prior. "Ever since auto class in high-school, I was interested. Ever since I bought my first car at 18, I've worked on my own vehicles. I always wanted an R32-R34. I wanted a more practical vehicle for day-to-day and family needs. I fell in love with the Stagea. It has been tuned for pump gas & E85. Puts down 350 HP at the wheels. Went in making 120 HP at the wheels. I am building the car up to make and handle 500 HP at the wheels. The next step is drivetrain including brakes, and then I will start planning the engine overhaul, and eventually racing it at Friday Night Street Legals. So far, this is our first road trip after getting the tuning done, feeling the roughly 3x the difference in the car. It was a smoother, faster drive. My love of JDM cars stems from late nights at the local Tim Hortons. Fifteen years ago, many of my friends at the time were not family bound and had the Skylines, Silvias, and Supras. I had children by 20, so sports cars were not possible. Fast forward to today, I realized why I could not keep a vehicle for more then one year, until I found my unicorn. It was the car I was meant to have. It's the only car I want to keep forever."

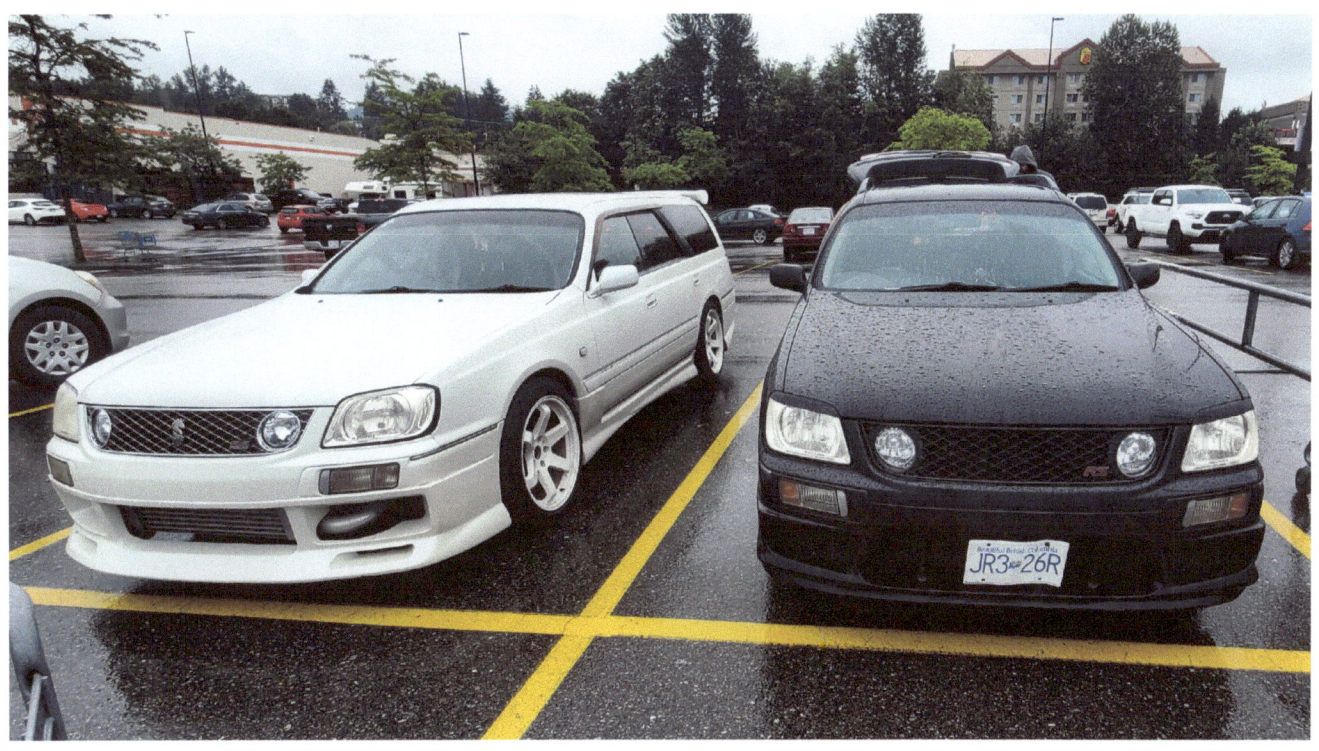

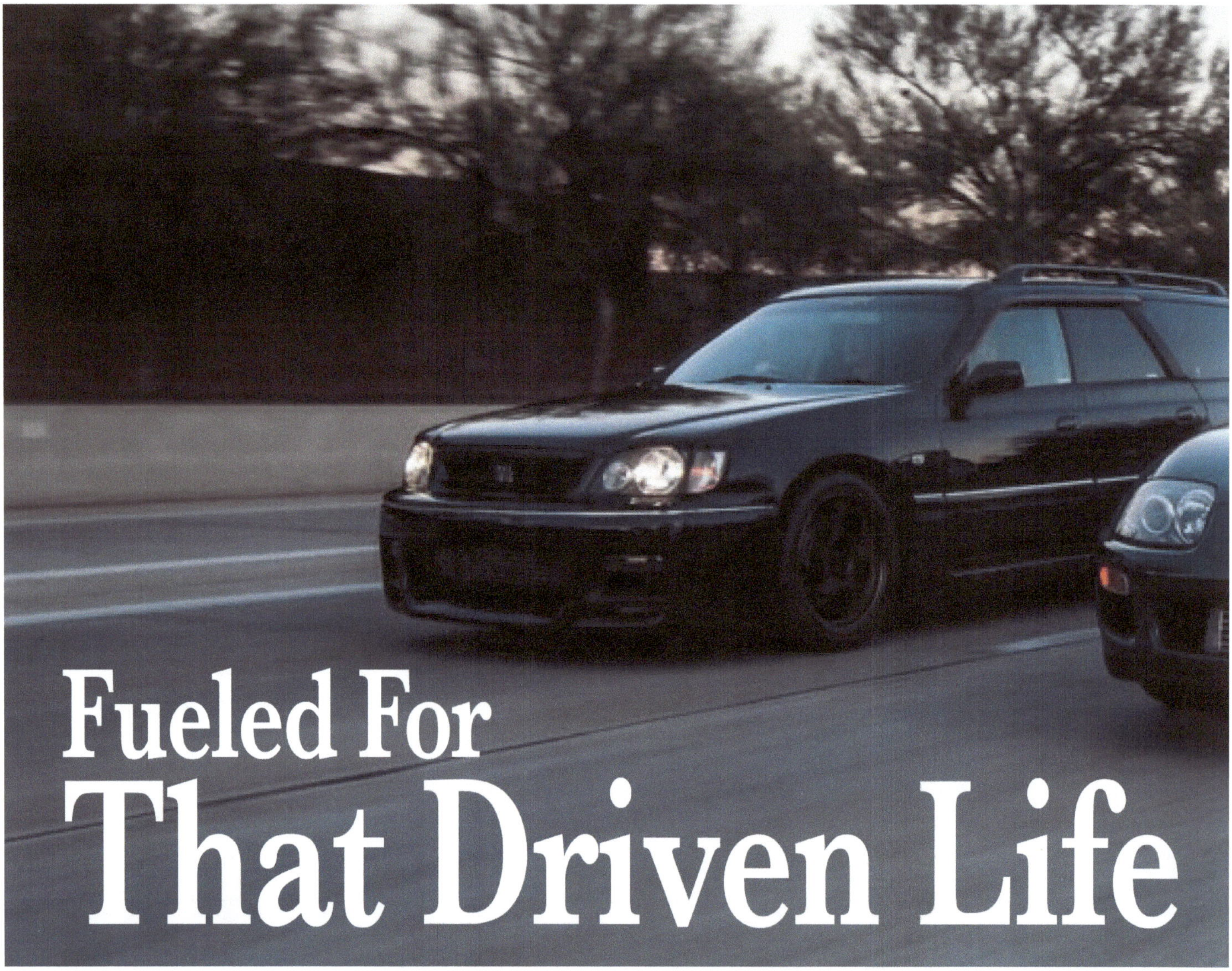

Fueled For
That Driven Life

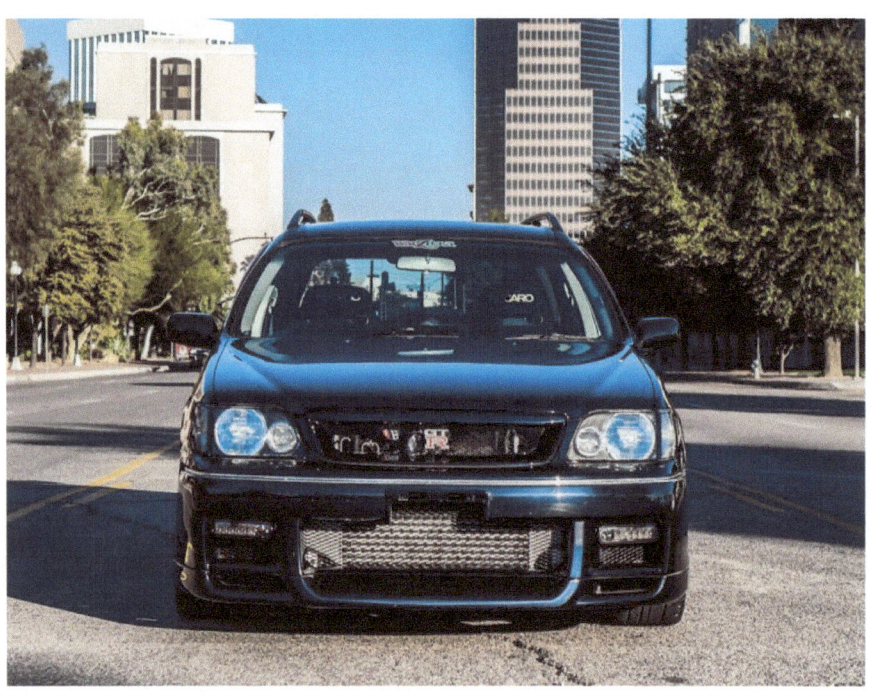

James imported his 1998 Nissan Stagea 260RS Autech November 2007. He chose the Stagea because they are tall, and he wasn't able to get his kids in a Supra. During a big car show, James says that a guy once said that his car is fake. They must not have heard of a Skyline wagon before! "I'm still waiting for my car to be legal in the USA. Someday, maybe."

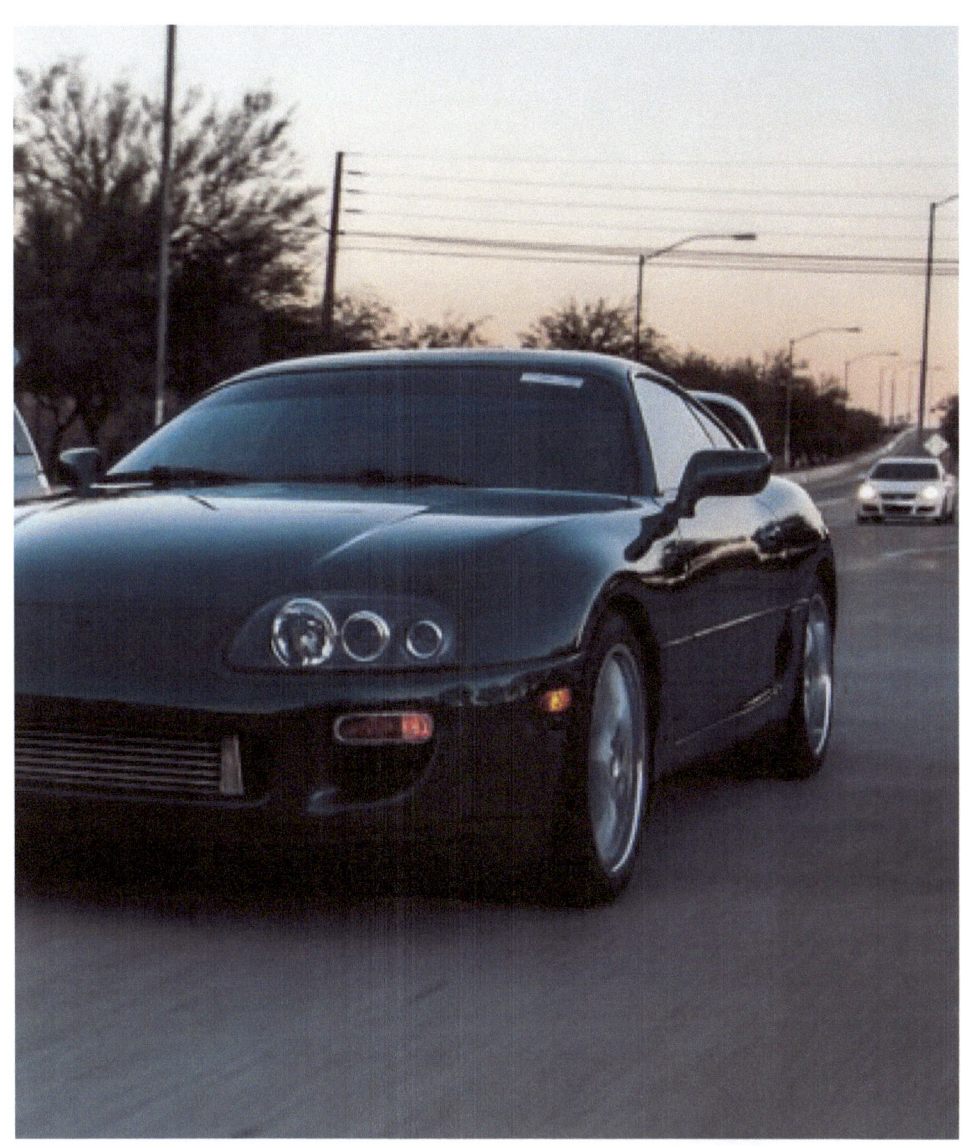

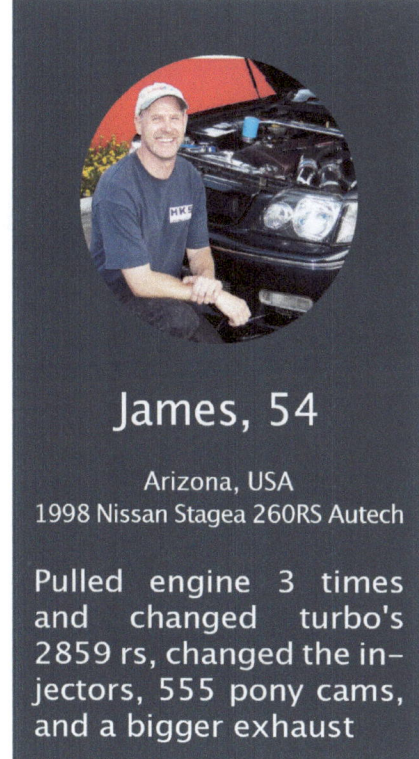

James, 54

Arizona, USA
1998 Nissan Stagea 260RS Autech

Pulled engine 3 times and changed turbo's 2859 rs, changed the injectors, 555 pony cams, and a bigger exhaust

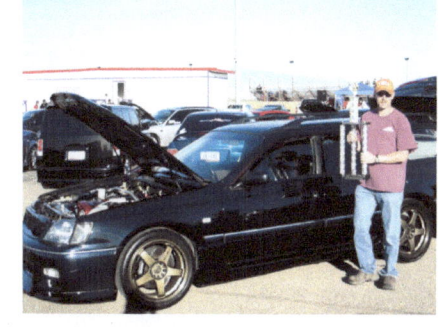

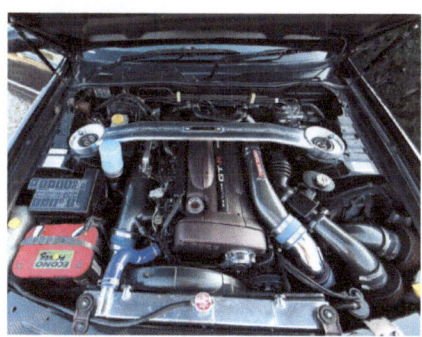

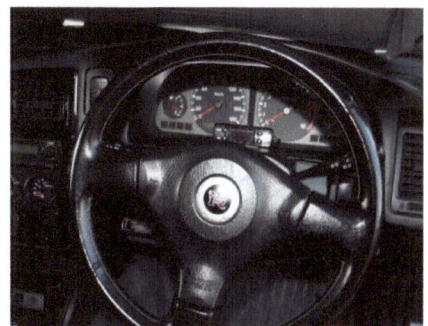

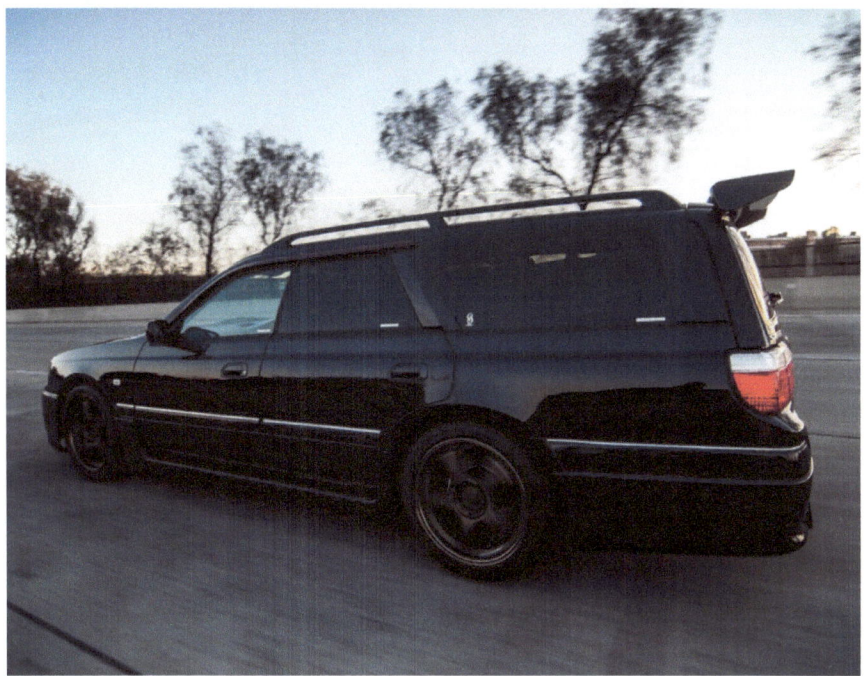

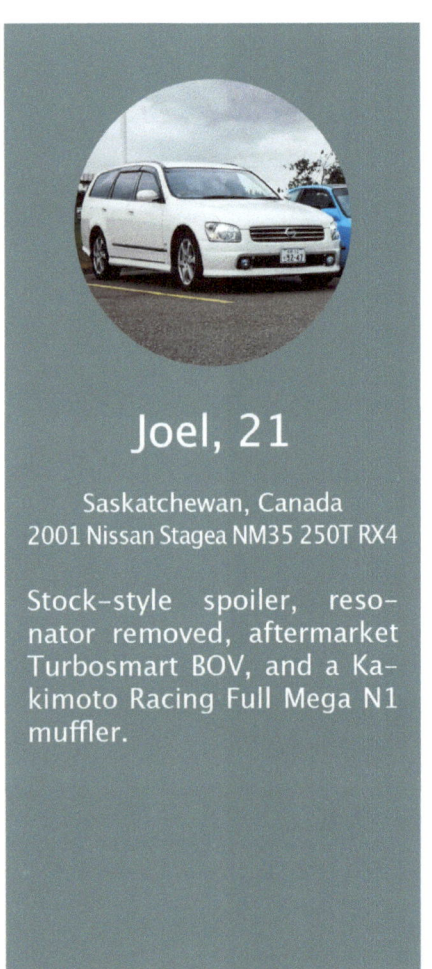

Joel, 21

Saskatchewan, Canada
2001 Nissan Stagea NM35 250T RX4

Stock-style spoiler, resonator removed, aftermarket Turbosmart BOV, and a Kakimoto Racing Full Mega N1 muffler.

Joel bought his 2001 Nissan Stagea NM35 250T RX4 as a birthday gift for himself locally from someone that he knew from school. "Like a lot of people, the Fast & Furious movies played a big part, but my family has always been into cars, so I was raised with cars always being a topic at the table. I wanted something not many people have. I wanted to stand out, and I sure do. Also, for the space these cars offer, I mean who else can say they put five pallets in the back of their car? It's awesome! And the fact that they are based on the Skyline I thought was cool." Joel has lowering springs that he plans to install soon, and in the near future, hopefully a set of rims, a wrap, aftermarket intercooler, air intake, grill, and maybe a front bumper at some point. "So far, my favorite memory is taking my friends for the first ride and doing a launch sending them to the back of their seats saying (oh damn) wasn't expecting that."

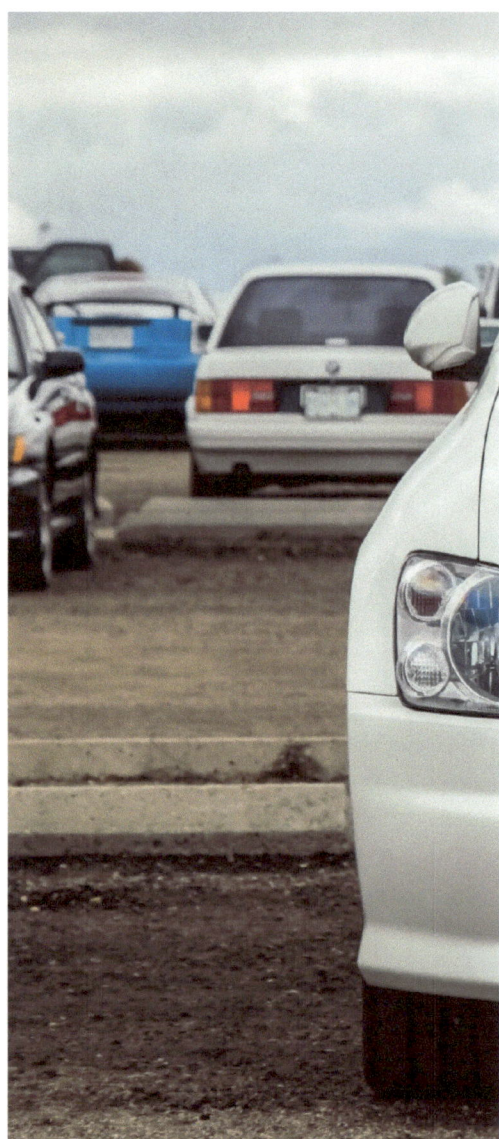

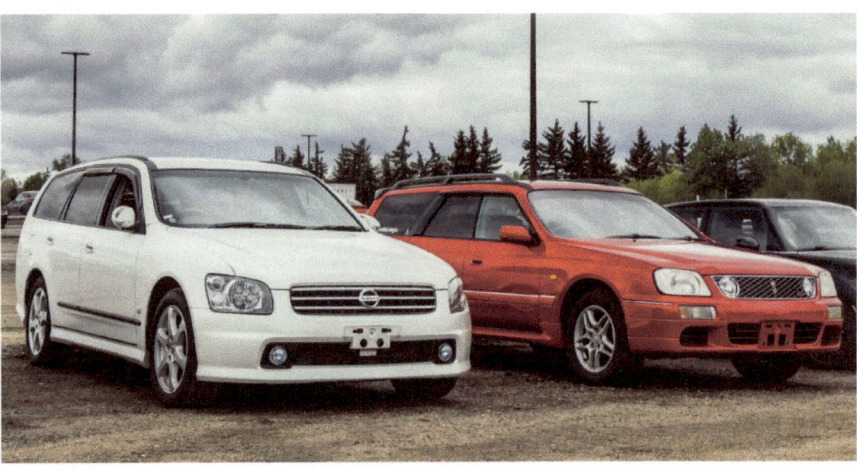

Clean Slate

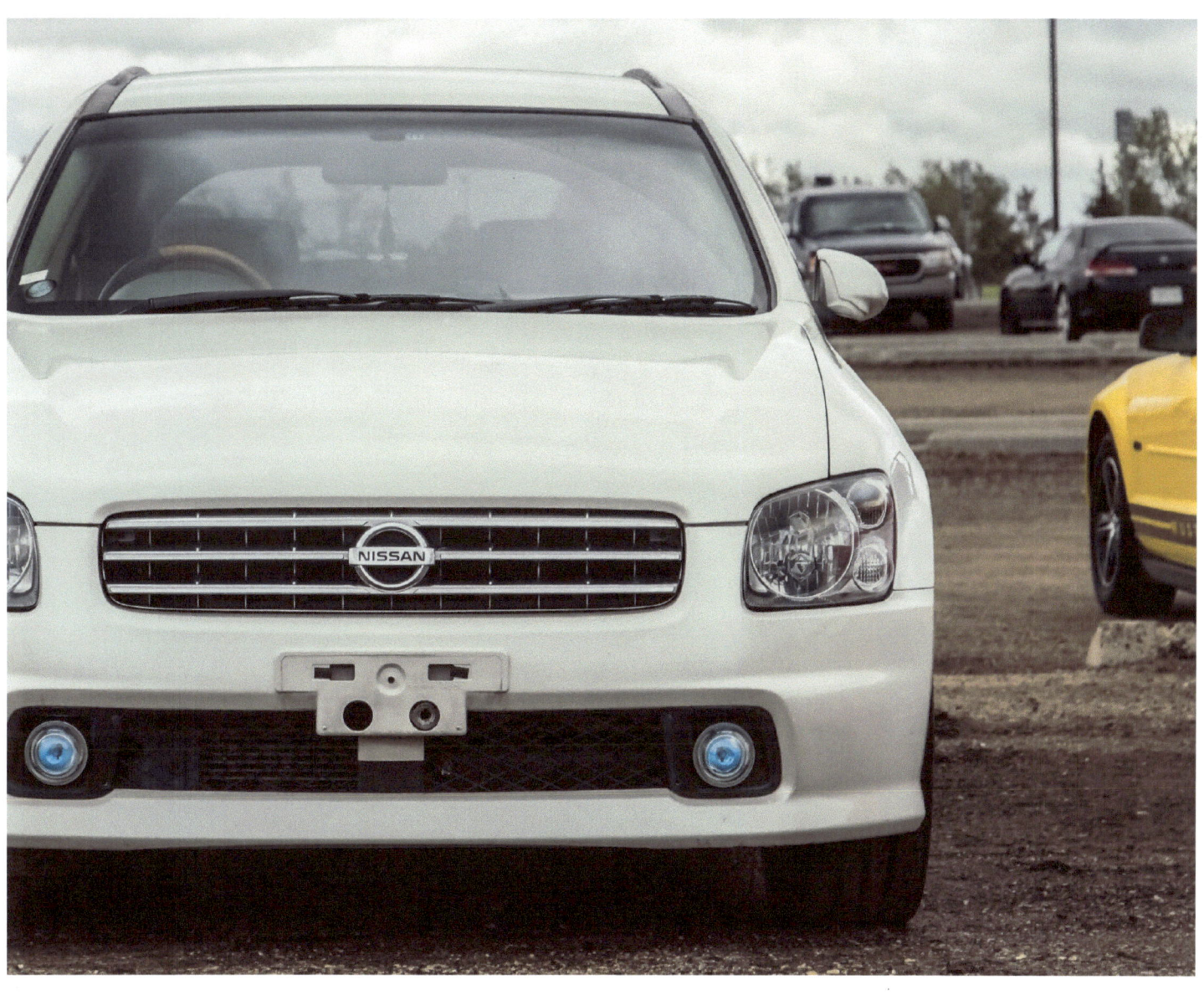

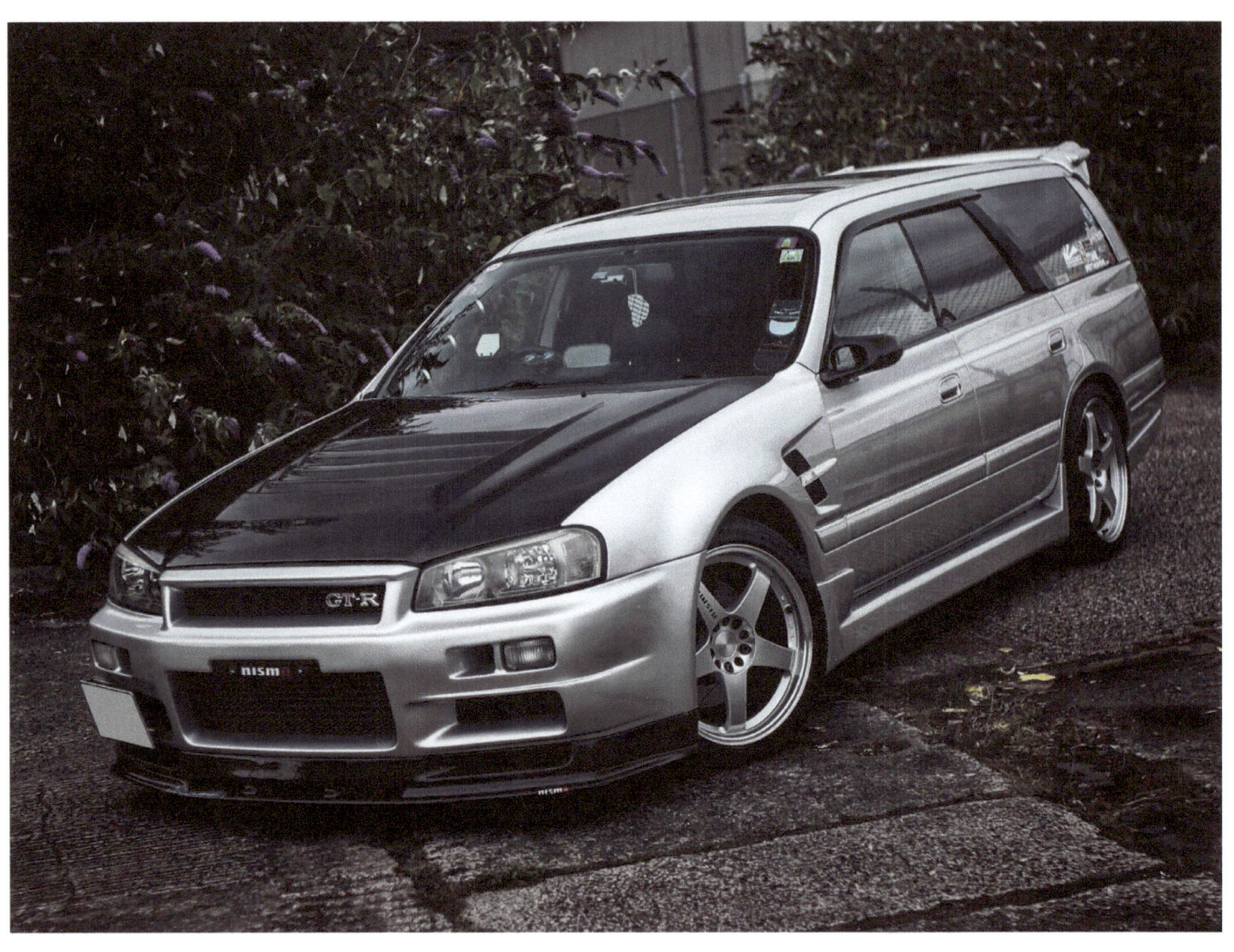

NEW CLASS

Jonathan imported his 1997 Nissan Stagea RS4 13 years ago. His father had first gotten him into cars. "I chose the Stagea as I've always liked wagons more, and one with an RB engine, I had to have one." One of his favorite memories with his Stagea was doing the Modball Rally, a 6000 mile race/rally from Ireland to Slovakia! "Crazy fun times, especially the Autobahn."

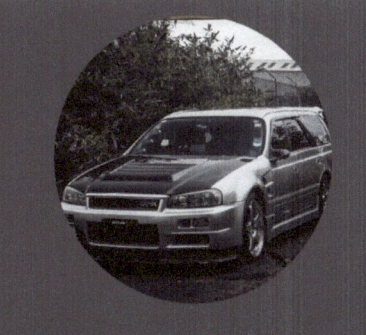

Jonathan, 39

Ireland
1997 Nissan Stagea RS4

Full Masa M34R kit, Abflug spoiler, Takeros boot extension, Dolphin sideskirts, Vspec wings, Seibon Vspec carbon bonnet, Vspec carbon lower lip and splitter, Carbon ganador mirrors, Rays Nismo LMGT4 wheels, R33 GTR Brembo brakes, BDA rotors, Ferodo pads, Project Mu pads, Titanium shims, Series 2 rear lights, Tomiei forged rods, CP forged pistons, race bearings, ARP crank & head bolts, N1 water pump, N1 oil pump, Walbro 450 fuel pump, Aeroflow fuel lines, Taarks fuel rail, Bosch 1200cc injectors, ARD custom alternator, Link G4+ ecu, R33 GTR 4WD ecu, R33 GTR transmission, Nismo Coppermix twin plate competition spec clutch, R31 cam covers, Garret GTX 3071R Owen's developments turbo, Wiring Specialties loom, HKS titanium hi-power exhaust, HKS intake and piping, HKS oil filter, HKS timing belt, Boost Junky's engine hoses, Samco radiator hoses, Greddy radiator, Greddy intercooler and piping, Greddy oil cooler, full cosmetic engine gasket kit, Audi R8 coils & custom loom, Cusco strut brace, Cusco catch can, DayZ full carbon dash, door finishers, Defi link gauges, boost, oil temp & oil pressure, Defi link heads up display, Defi link display, Innovative wideband gauge, Plex usdm info meter gauge, carbon dash gauge surround, Nardi steering wheel, Nismo mats, Nismo quick shift & gearstick, Cusco rear strut brace, Kenwood double din radio, JL Audio front components, Kenwood 3 way coaxials, Vibe active sub

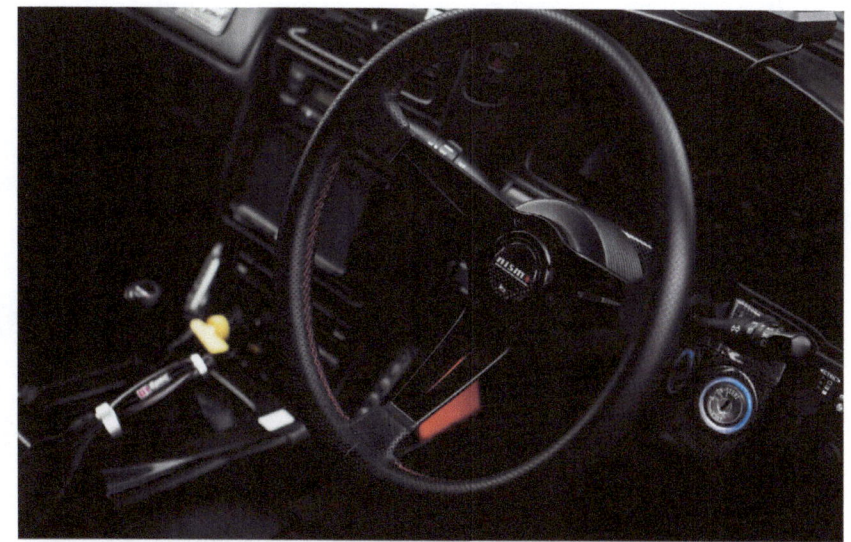

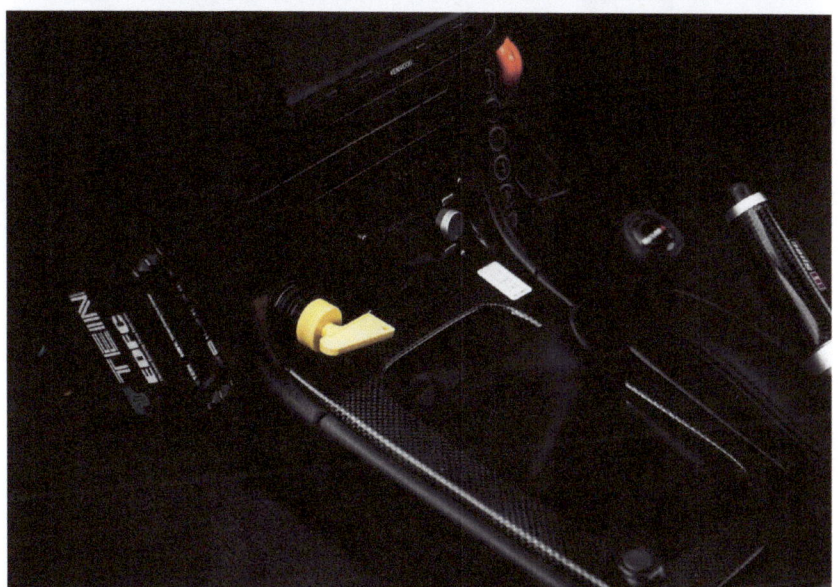

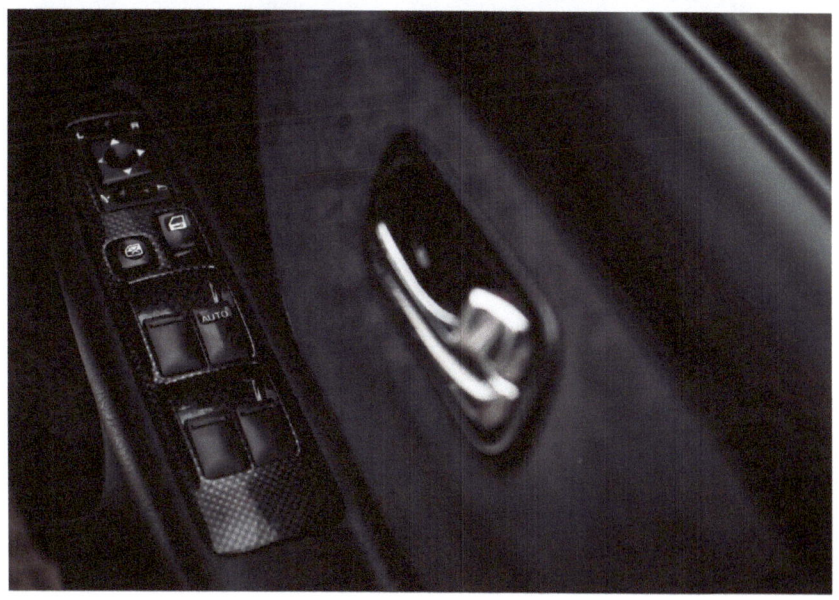

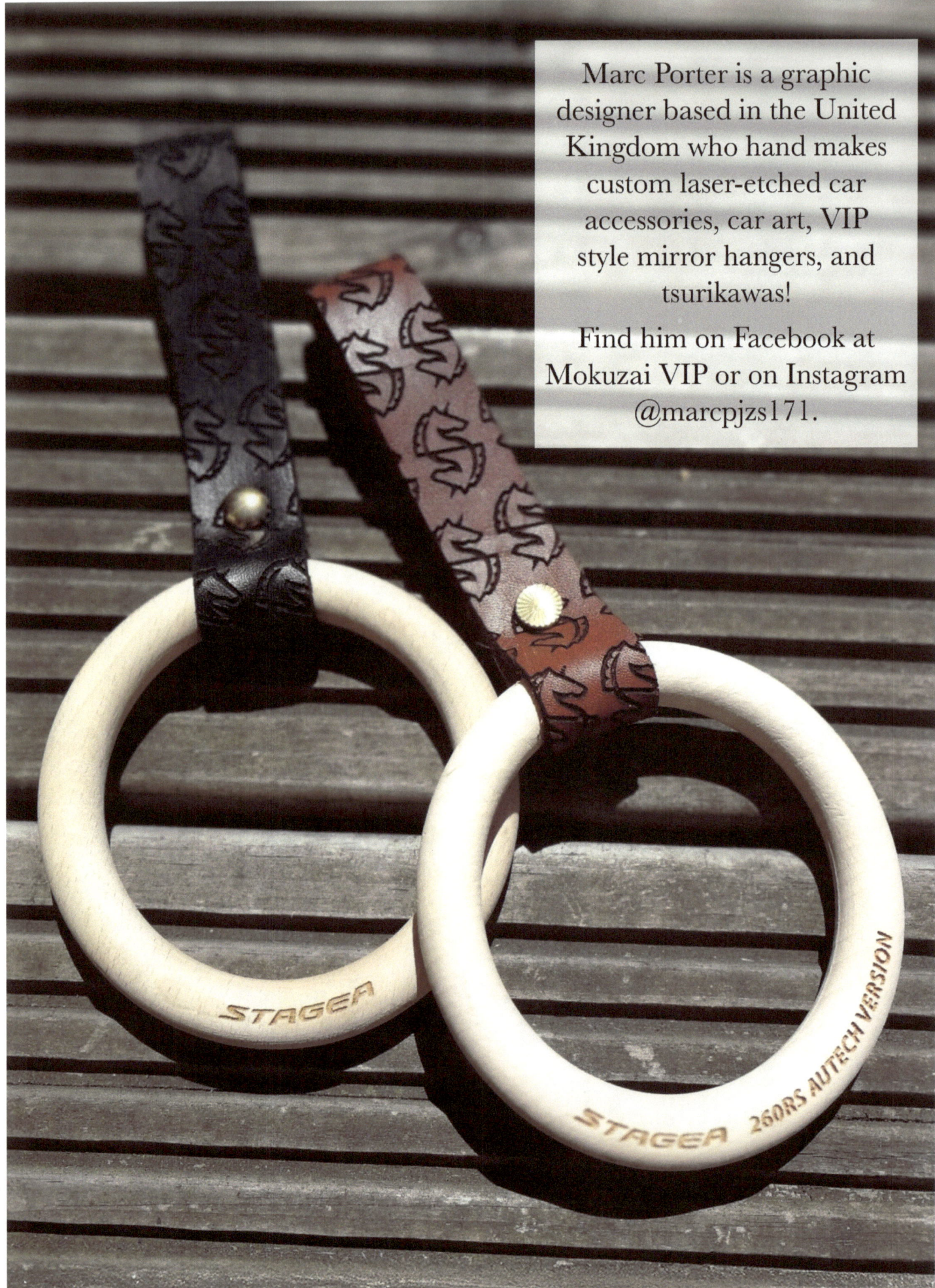

www.ingramcontent.com/pod-product-compliance
Lightning Source LLC
Chambersburg PA
CBHW051837210526
45473CB00005B/1919

@officialhollidbarzz

@brandicedaniel

@alimanning_

8

NATALIE BIRDSONG

@iamhairbynatalieb

10

MARCUS D PORTER

@marcusdporterstudios

12

SACK CHASER TM

@sackchaserdt

14

AALIYAH JOHNSON

@he_turned_it

16

SLNP KRIS

@queenari_97

18

ADVERTISE WITH US

HOLLI D BARZZ

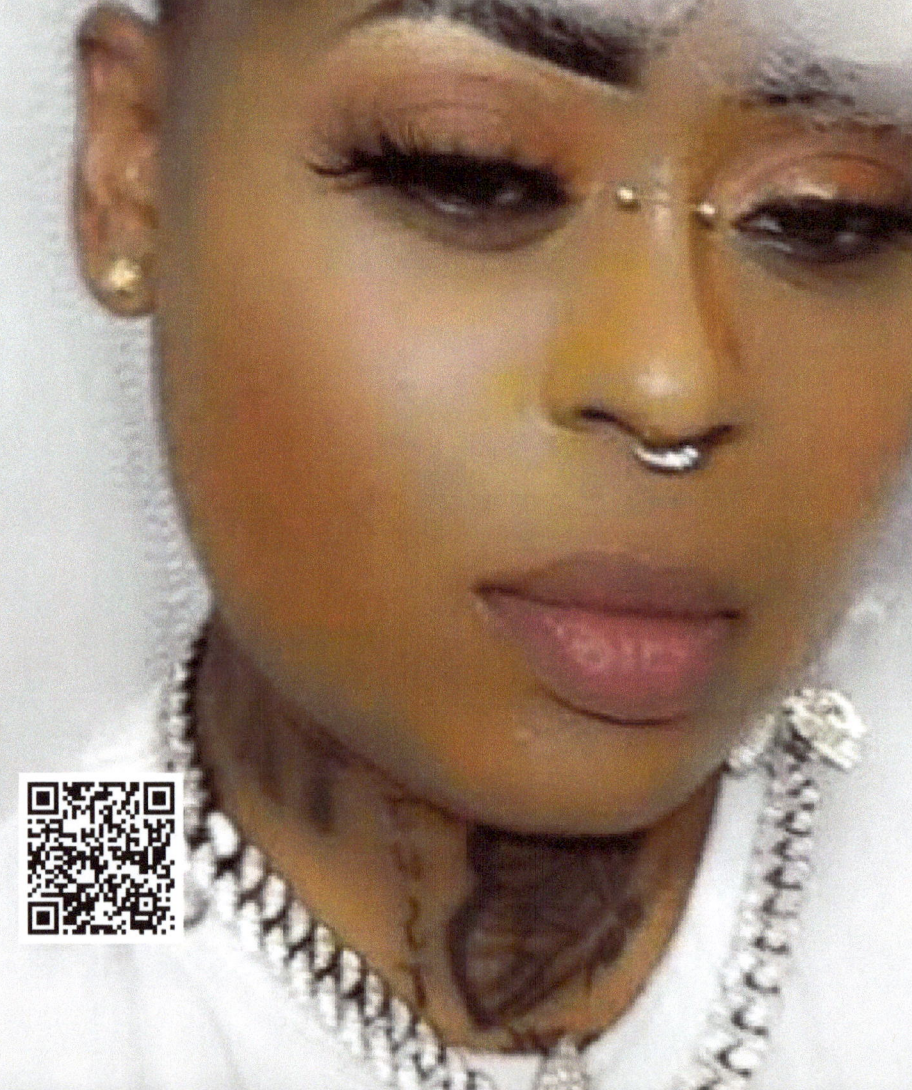

HOLLI D BARZZ: A RISING STAR OF CHICAGO'S LOW END

Holli D Barzz is a rising star in Chicago's bustling music industry. She has charmed audiences with her raw talent and thrilling performances despite coming from the city's poorest neighborhoods. Holli D Barzz has established herself as one of Chicago's most promising performers, having received numerous award nominations, including the prestigious 2024 Best Live Performer of the Year at the 312 Music Awards.

Her versatility and proficiency in hip-hop have won her three iLLY Award nominations, which recognize her contributions to the genre, infectious stage presence, and unmistakable charisma. Holli D Barzz's music has adorned the airwaves of several radio stations, earning widespread recognition and establishing her as a force to be reckoned with in the music business.

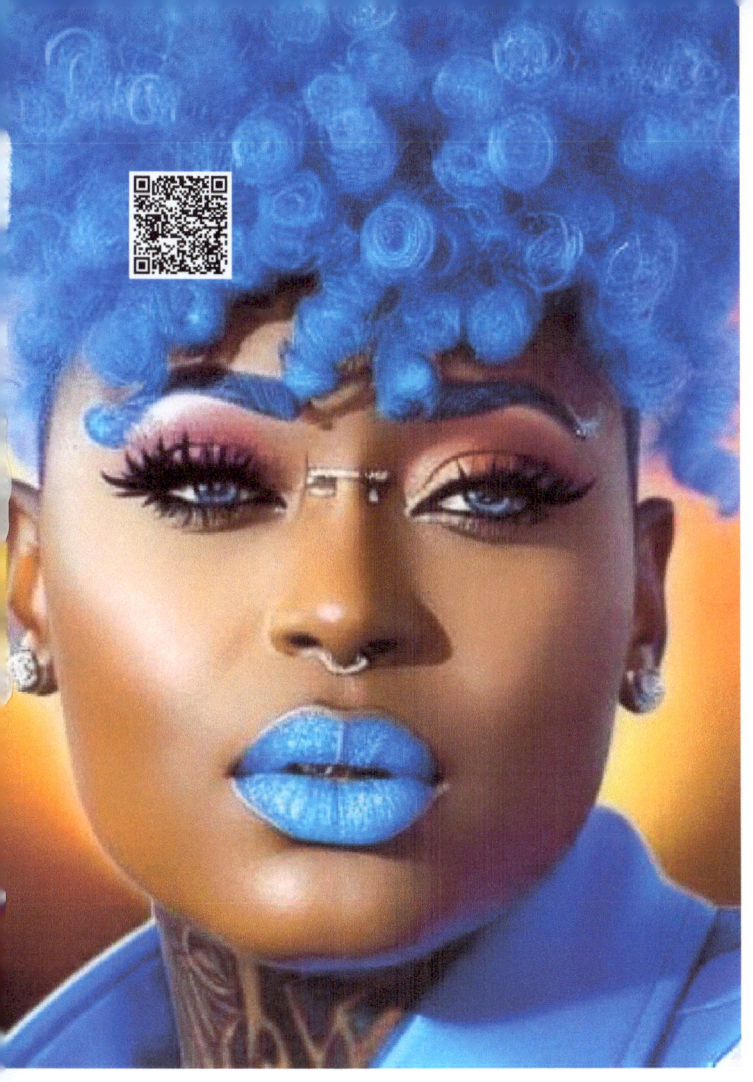
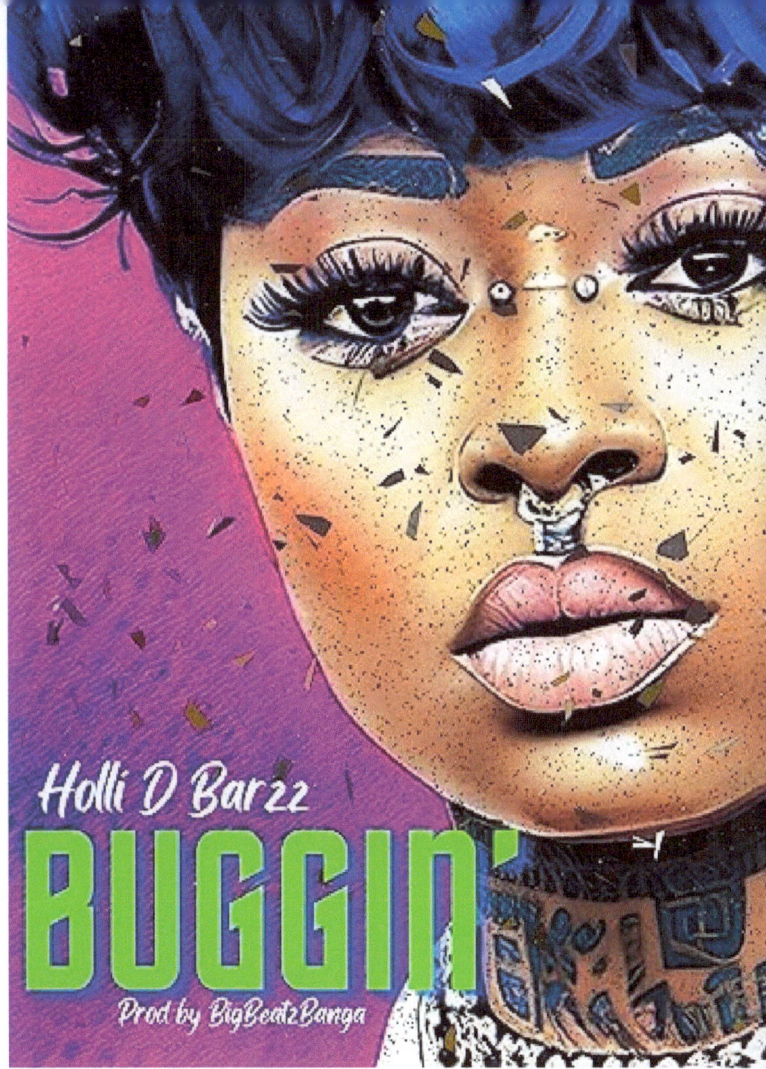

From intimate clubs to bustling bars and lounges, Holli D Barzz has left her mark on the Chicagoland area with her dynamic performances. Her stage presence is unmatched, drawing audiences into her world with every lyric and beat.

In addition to her musical abilities, Holli D Barzz has made an impression in the media, with appearances on major platforms like as RawRadio and Meli P's Playground. Her charismatic personality and intelligent analysis have won over fans and critics alike, confirming her place as a rising star in the field.

Not content with just performing on stage, Holli D Barzz has also demonstrated her lyrical talent in the competitive field of battle rap, competing against difficult opponents such as Niema Loca on Heat Check Live. With each performance, she pushes the boundaries of her profession, motivating both audiences and fellow artists with her love and dedication to her work. Keep an eye on Holli D Barzz as she continues to ascend in the music industry, embodying the talent and spirit of Chicago's South Side with each verse.

#YaaaYaaa #BarzzBitch

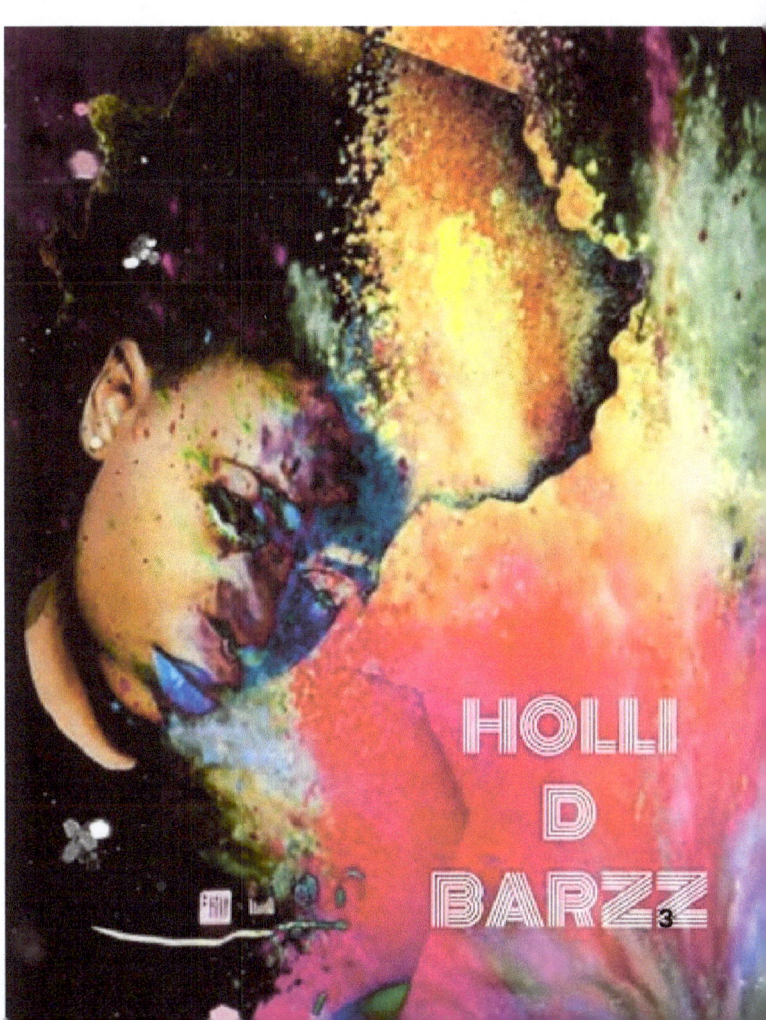

BRANDICE DANIEL

THE TRAILBLAZING FASHION ENTREPRENEUR WHO RUNS HARLEM FASHION ROW AND HFICON360. SHE IS KNOWN FOR HER INVENTIVENESS AND COLLABORATIONS WITH INDUSTRY TITANS SUCH AS DAPPER DAN AND TOMMY HILFIGER.

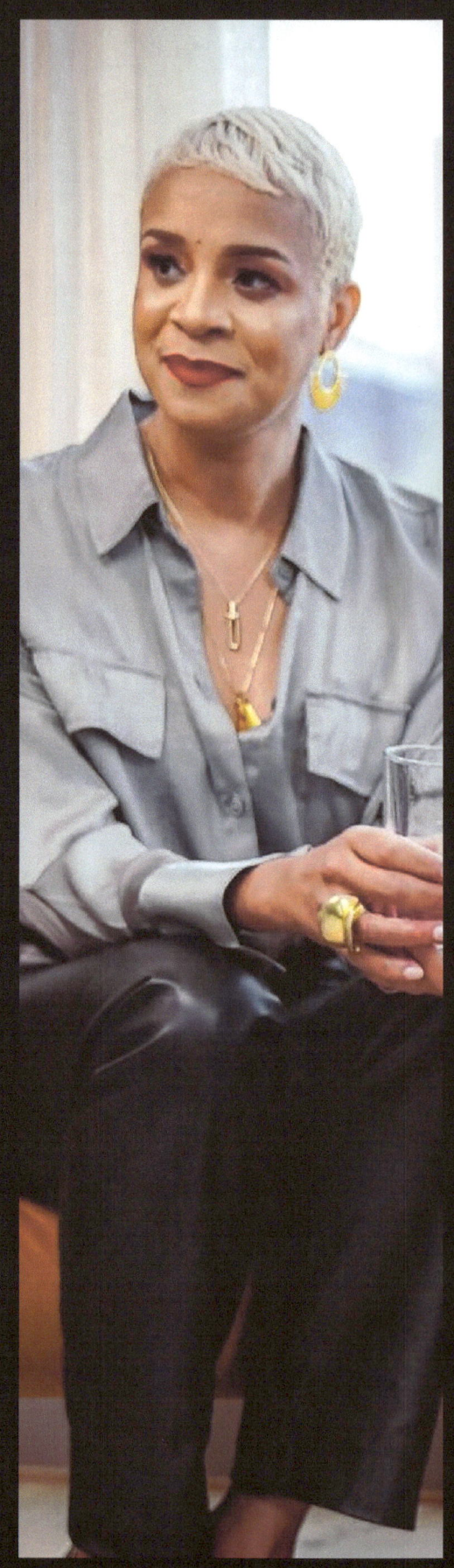

Brandice Daniel, a powerful figure in the fashion industry, originates from the energetic city of Memphis. She has taken the industry to new heights as the creator and impetus behind HFIcon360 and Harlem Fashion Row (HFR), all the while being loyal to her Southern origins. Brandice has established herself as a forerunner in the fashion industry by winning the respect and admiration of her peers with her sharp sense of style and inventiveness.

At the heart of Brandice's enterprise is Harlem Fashion Row, a platform dedicated to presenting minority designers and celebrating diversity in fashion. HFR was founded on her love for diversity and representation, and it has become a beacon of empowerment, giving marginalized voices a platform to shine. Brandice's leadership has not only altered the fashion world, but has also created a sense of community and belonging inside the industry.

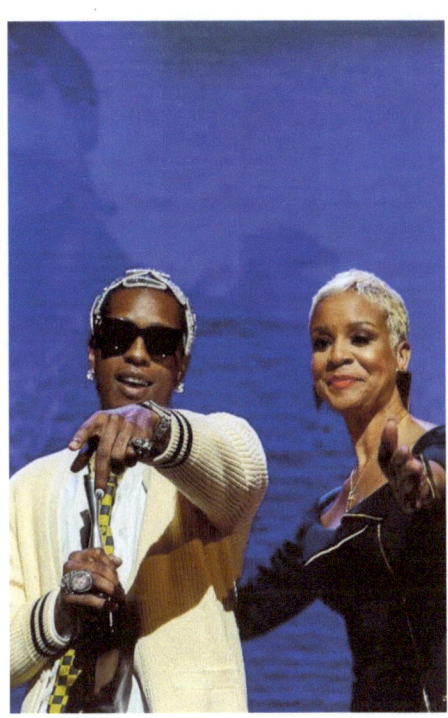 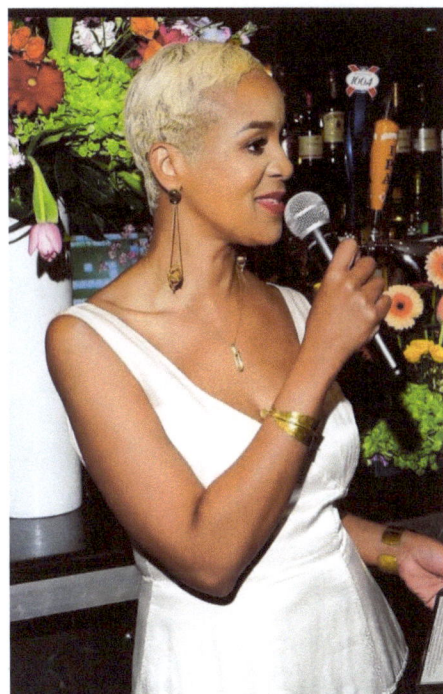 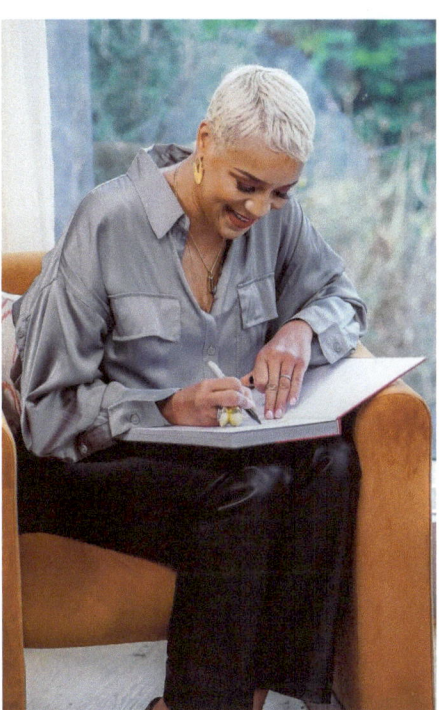

With HFIcon360, Brandice has solidified her reputation as a visionary entrepreneur. By leveraging technology, she has created immersive experiences that bridge the gap between brands and consumers. Her collaborations with giants such as Dapper Dan and Tommy Hilfiger have pushed the envelope of creativity, fusing streetwear culture with high fashion in unforeseen ways.

espite her global success, Brandice stays firmly linked to her Memphis roots, using her platform to promote her city and new talent in the area. Through her charity activities and mentorship programs, she continues to develop the next generation of designers, ensuring that Memphis remains a thriving center of creativity and innovation in the fashion industry.

In a world where trends come and go, Brandice Daniel's imprint endures. Her persistent devotion to diversity, creativity, and community inspires and empowers those around her, creating an unforgettable effect on the fashion industry and beyond.

Ali Manning

"From Food Science to Heartfelt Stories, Memphis' Culinary Renaissance Woman"

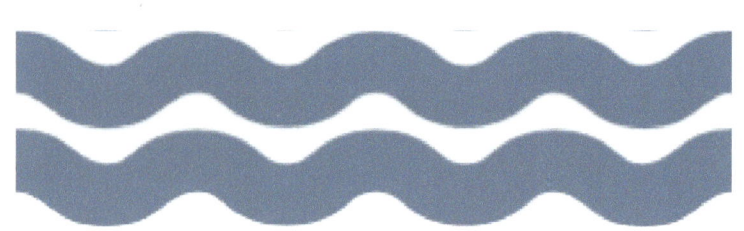

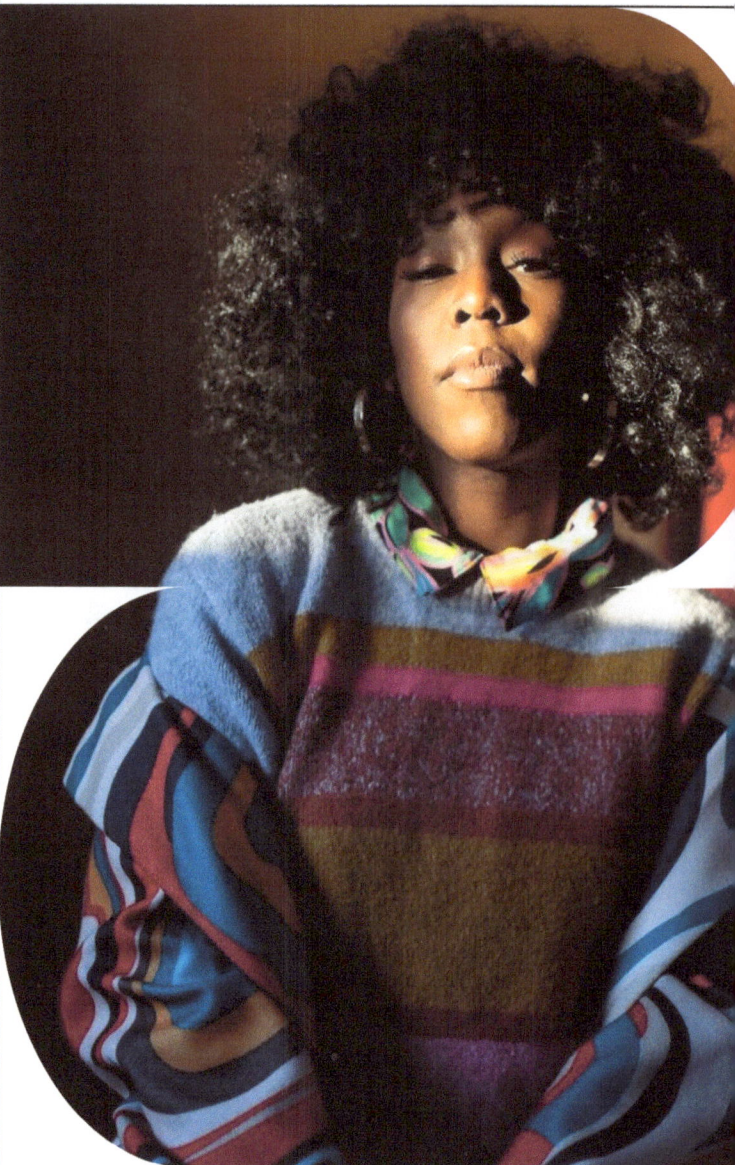

Ali Manning exemplifies versatility, flawlessly combining her passions for culinary science, consulting, literature, and art. Ali, who hails from the dynamic city of Memphis, has received international appreciation for her multifarious talents, propelling her to platforms such as Netflix's "Snack vs Chef." She dazzles audiences with her expertise, engaging in culinary showdowns that demonstrate her unique approach to cuisine.

Beyond the screen, Ali's literary achievements shine brightly, with her critically acclaimed book "Can I Play with My Food?" enthralling readers of all ages. She teaches vital lessons about acceptance through the adorable characters Nema and Lexi, illustrating that everything is possible with love. This beautiful story not only entertains but also teaches, demonstrating how playfulness may be combined with meaningful learning experiences.

Ali's influence extends beyond the pages of her book, as she appears on WMC5 Memphis, where she discusses culinary science and engaging activities for kids. Her riveting chats with hosts such as Gina Neely reveal the limitless possibilities of culinary discovery, generating a better respect for the science behind our favorite foods.

Ali Manning's tenacious spirit and unrelenting commitment to her profession continue to inspire and uplift, making an unforgettable impression on the culinary world and beyond. As a symbol of innovation and inclusivity, she embodies the transformational power of passion and tenacity, demonstrating that true achievement has no boundaries.

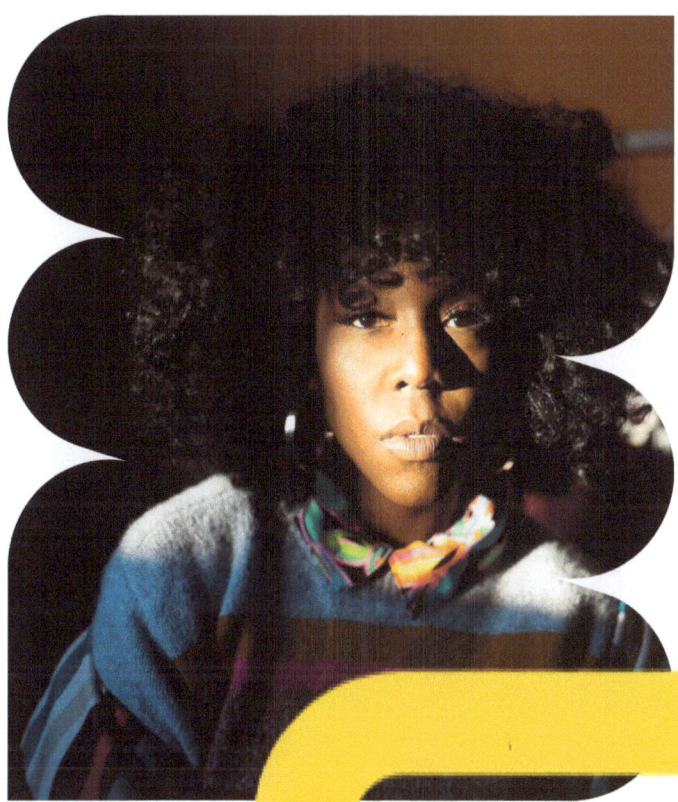
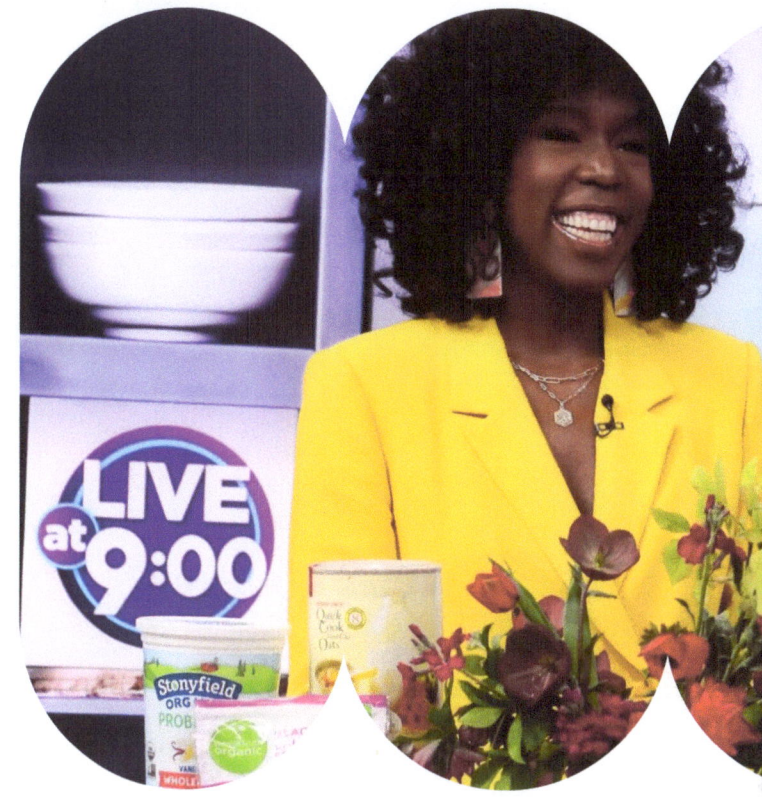
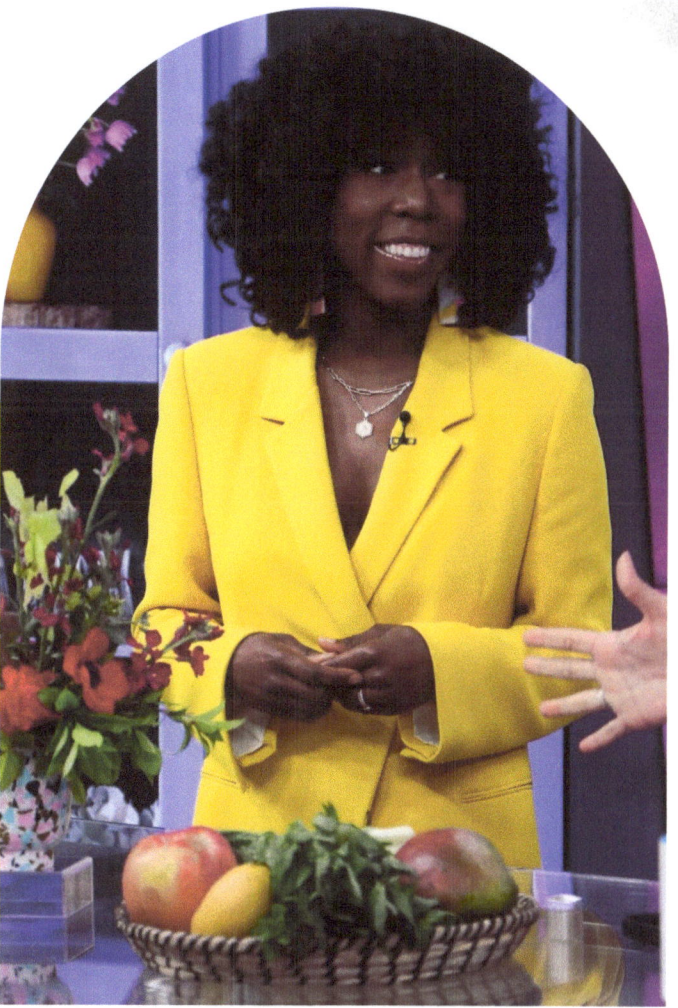

NATALIE BIRDSONG

By Margarita Perez
Photography by Francois Mercer

A SHORT INTRO OR KICKER OF THE ARTICLE WILL GO HERE.

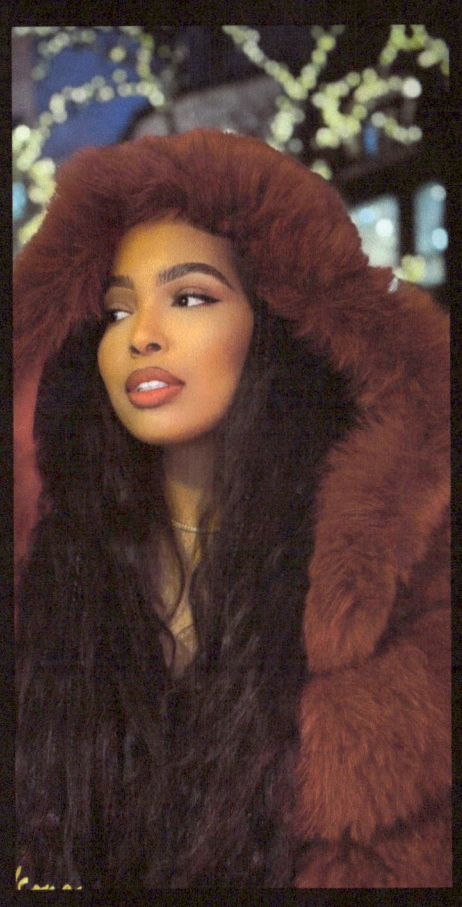

Natalie Birdsong is a shining example of innovation and quality in the beauty and entrepreneurial industries in Chicago. Natalie is a famous hairstylist, entrepreneur, bestselling author, and fascinating public speaker whose career has been marked by passion, determination, and unmatched talent. Now, as she seeks to expand her empire, Natalie is looking for top-tier talent, such as professional hairstylists, wig frontal specialists, and talented locticians, to join her distinguished team.

Natalie's imaginative approach revolves around her groundbreaking book and course, "Million Dollar Hairstylist," which is a definitive roadmap to attaining extraordinary success in the hair industry. Her comprehensive courses offer her wealth of experience and expertise, putting aspiring stylists on the path to establishing a seven-figure empire from the ground up. Her unique combination of commercial acumen and artistic flair enables individuals to reach their full potential and achieve their entrepreneurial goals.

Aside from her literary and educational activities, Natalie captivates audiences all over the world with her exciting public speaking ability. She sparks the flames of desire and promise in everyone who have the opportunity of hearing her speak, using inspiring anecdotes and useful insights gained from her own journey.

Her legacy as a trailblazer and mentor grows stronger as she pushes the boundaries of creativity and enterprise farther. Natalie, with an uncompromising commitment to perfection and a vision for the future, welcomes aspiring hairstylists and beauty aficionados to join her on the exhilarating journey to realize their goals of success in the dynamic world of hairstyling.

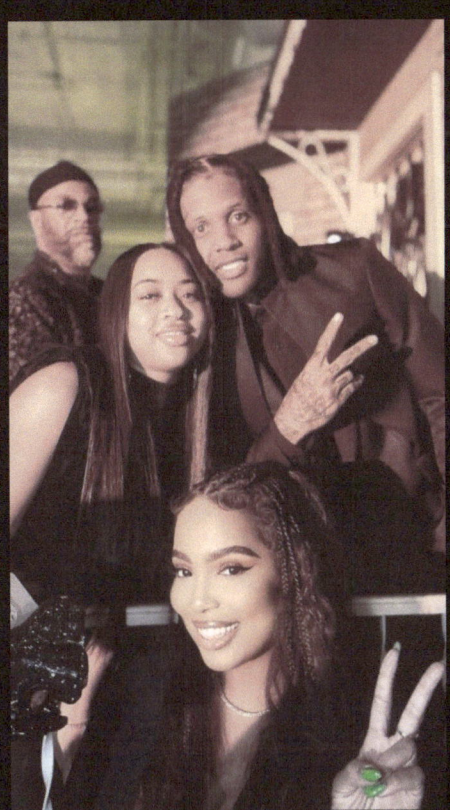

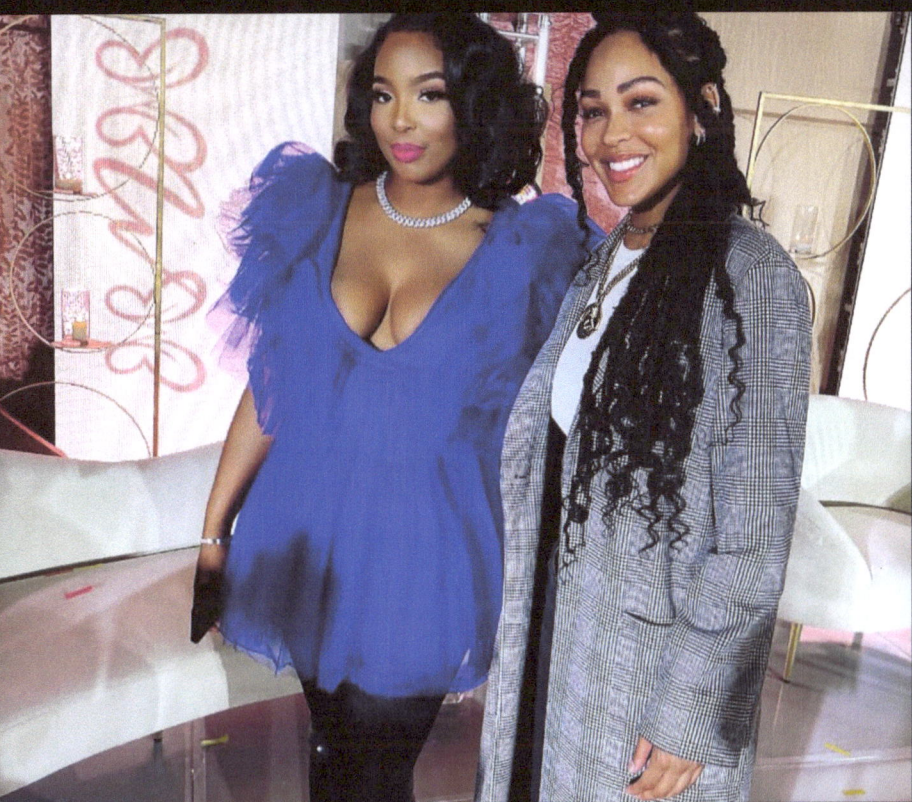

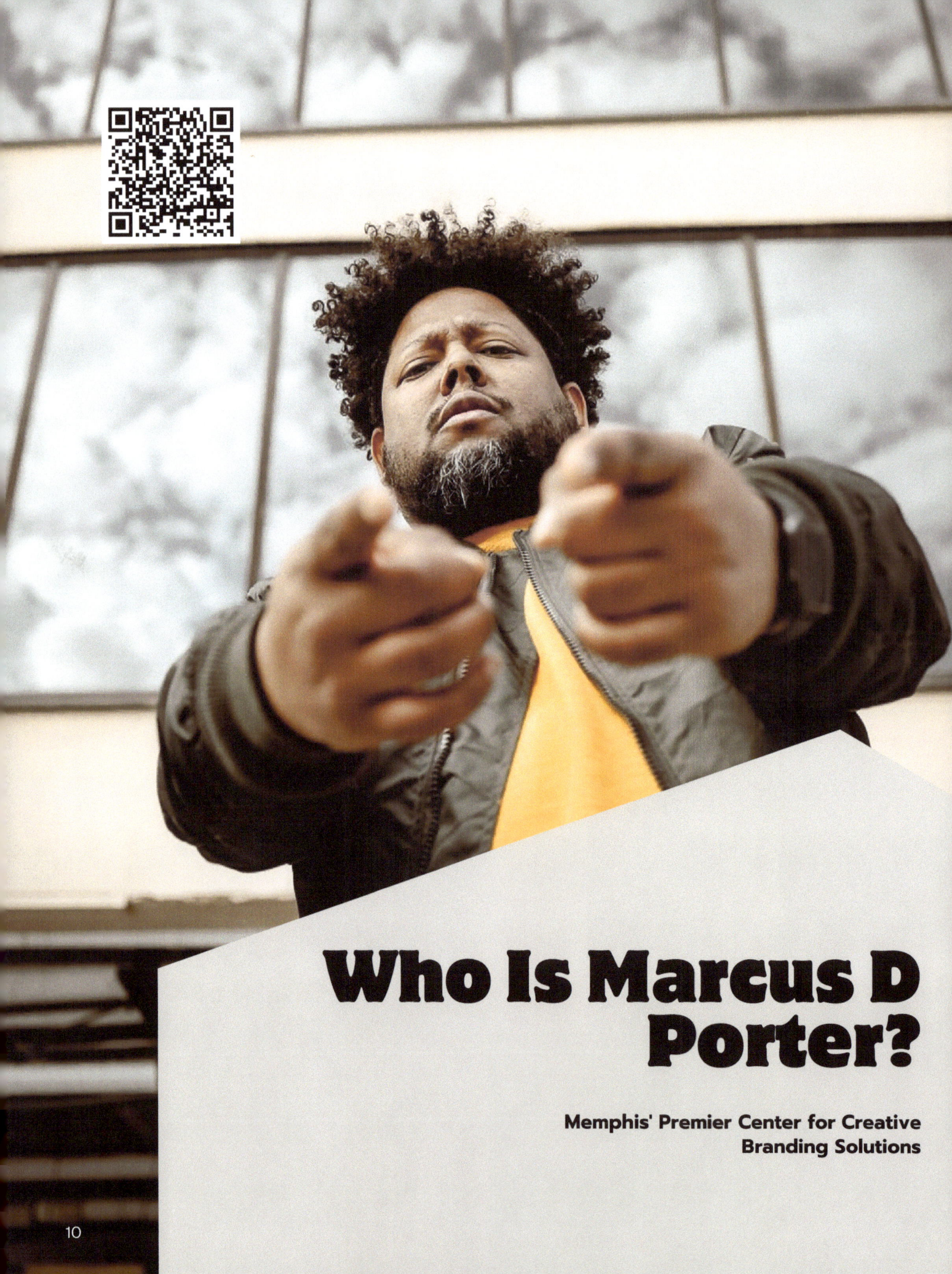

Who Is Marcus D Porter?

Memphis' Premier Center for Creative Branding Solutions

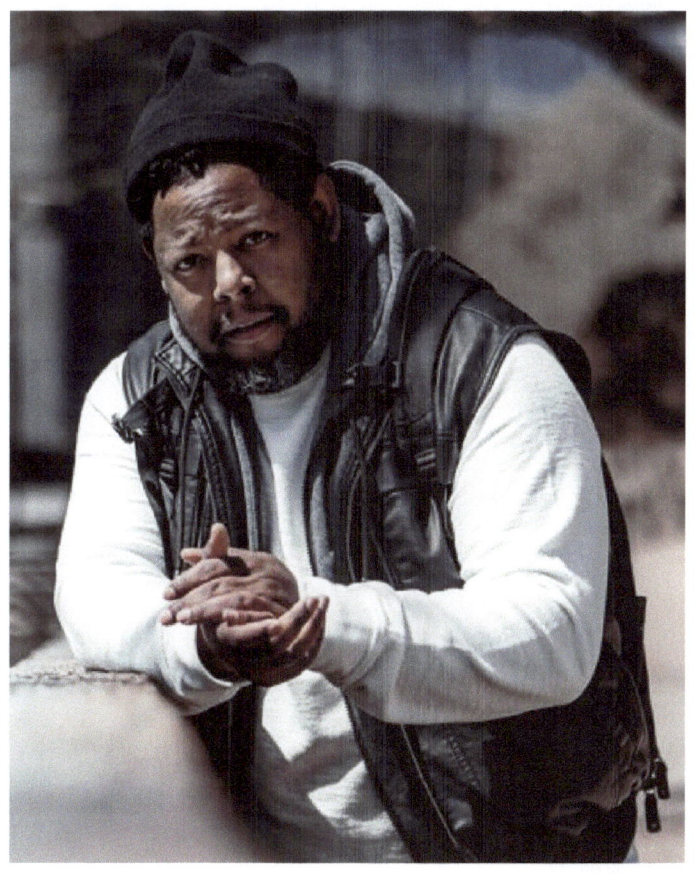 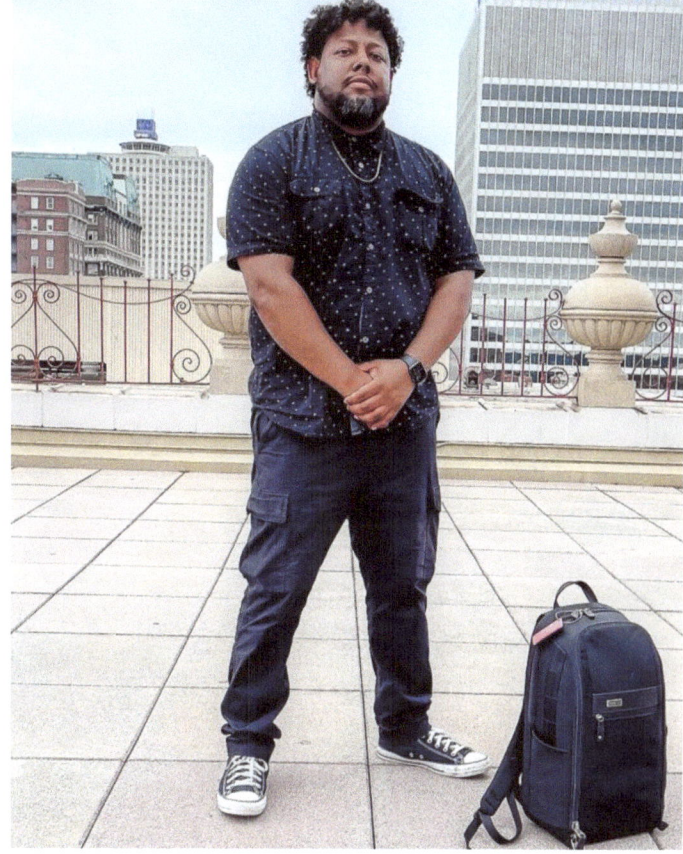

Marcus D Porter Studios, located in the center of Memphis, is a leading location for businesses looking to boost their brand presence through appealing imagery and storytelling. This studio, led by the versatile talent Marcus D Porter, is more than simply a venue; it's a nexus of creativity, innovation, and digital marketing knowledge. Marcus' varied skill set includes photography, cinematography, digital marketing, and influencer outreach, allowing businesses and company owners to create content that not only sells but also resonates deeply with their target audience.

His aim goes beyond simply taking photographs; it's about producing stories that elicit emotion, pique curiosity, and leave an indelible impact. Marcus works together with clients to create personalized content that speaks to the spirit of their business while delivering practical outcomes. Marcus D Porter Studios is committed to helping businesses prosper in an increasingly competitive digital market, whether through gorgeous photography, fascinating videos, or engaging social media campaigns.

Aside from his work as a photographer and filmmaker, Marcus is a trusted counselor and influencer in the field of digital marketing. With a great awareness of developing trends and consumer behavior, he offers important advice to firms navigating the ever-changing environment of online marketing. He thought leadership and strategic alliances continue to help firms remain ahead of the competition and stand out in a crowded industry.

Marcus D Porter Studios, Memphis' go-to destination for premium video creation and digital marketing expertise, is more than a studio; it's a success catalyst, propelling organizations to new heights of visibility, engagement, and profitability. With Marcus at the helm, businesses can be confident that their content will not only sell, but also fascinate and inspire audiences throughout the world.

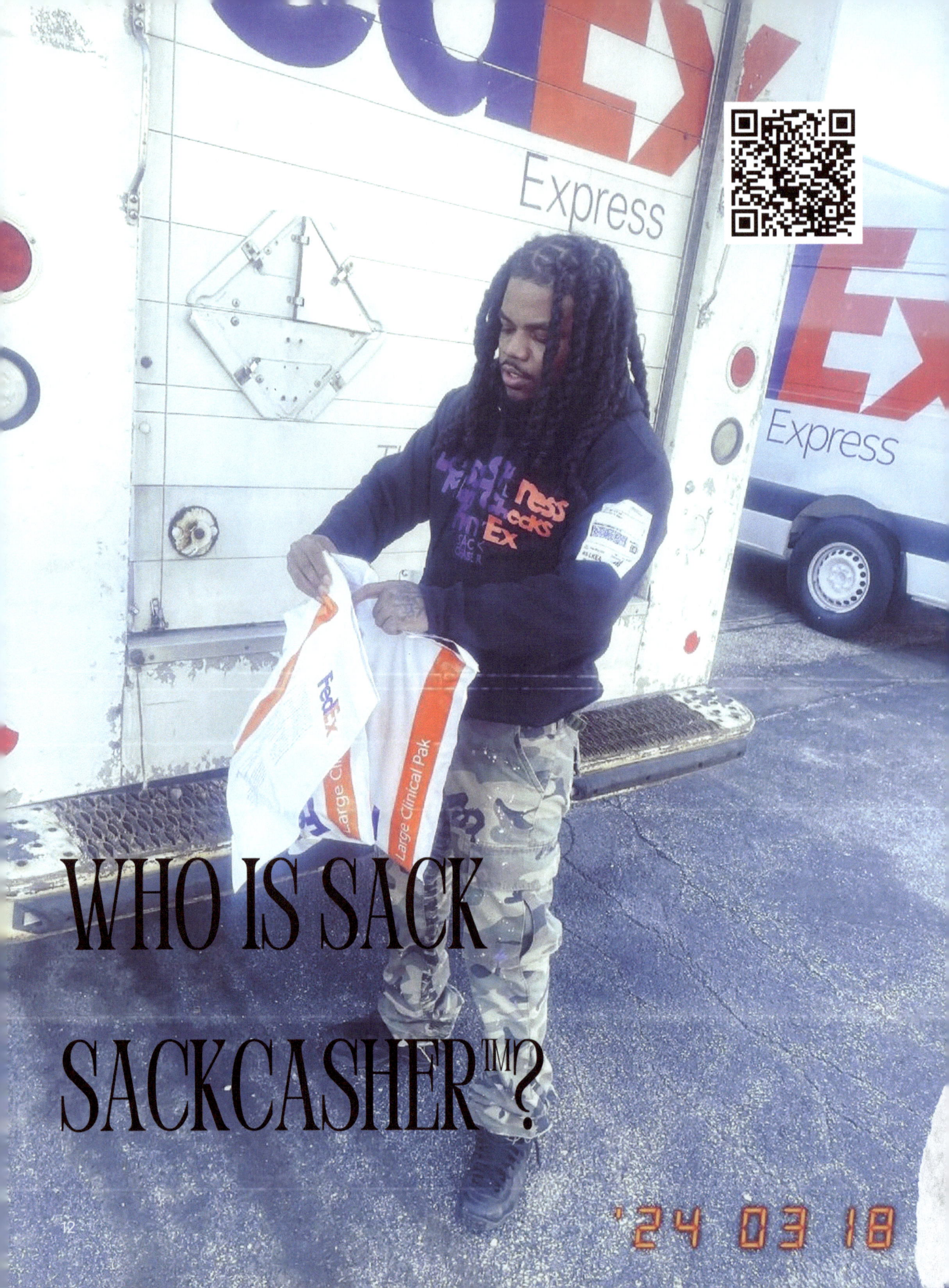

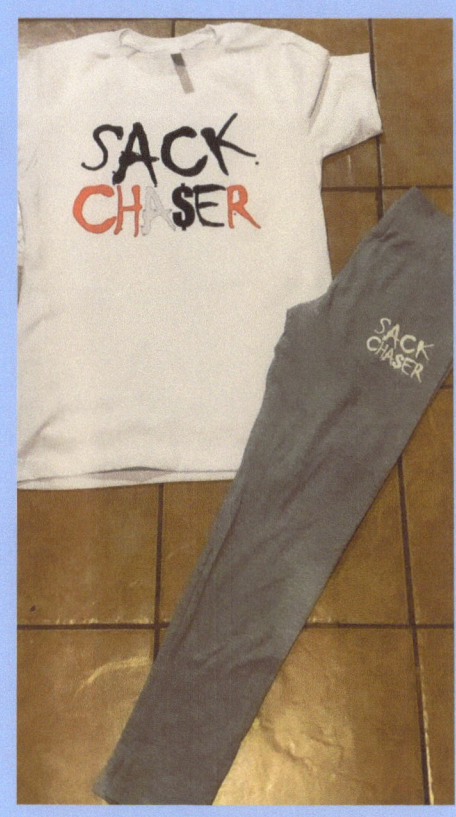

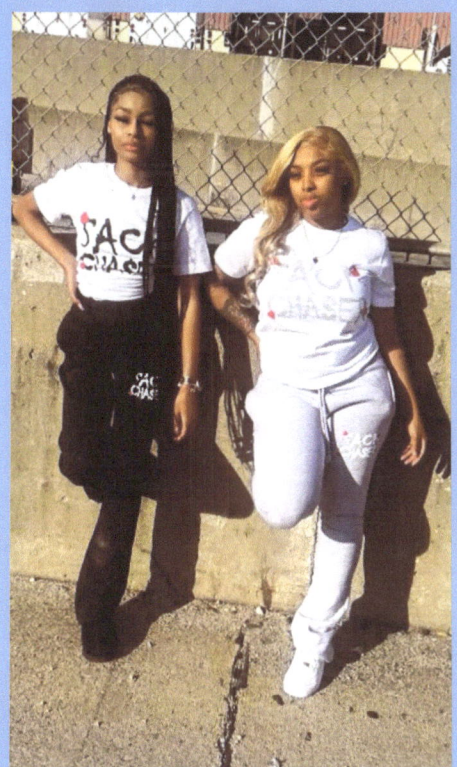

AIn the busy city of Chicago, Sack Chaser reigns supreme as a productive artist and imaginative fashion designer. With a dynamic blend of musical prowess and sartorial flair, he personifies Chicago's lively urban culture. Sack's latest sonic offering, "Play Your Part," exemplifies his range and originality, encapsulating the spirit of life in the fast lane with captivating beats and insightful lyrics.

Beyond his musical abilities, Sack Chaser is a true Renaissance man who channels his creative energy into the world of fashion. His clothes designs reflect his diverse style, which combines streetwear sensibility with high-fashion components to produce outfits that appeal to both urban trendsetters and fashion connoisseurs. From sleek sweatshirts embroidered with his trademark emblem to statement tees exuding attitude and flair, Sack's clothing captures the essence of modern-day cool.

PLAY YOUR PART," BY CHICAGO'S UP-AND-COMING MUSICAL AND FASHION STAR, SETS THE PACE

But perhaps what distinguishes Sack Chaser is his unrelenting dedication to his trade and community. As a devoted Chicagoan, he uses his platform to encourage and inspire others, fighting for social change and supporting the next generation of artists and entrepreneurs. Sack Chaser's music, fashion, and philanthropy continue to have an indelible effect on Chicago's cultural landscape and beyond.

So, whether he's releasing addictive beats in the studio or pushing the frontiers of style on the fashion catwalk, one thing is clear: Sack Chaser is a creative force to be reckoned with, and his star is only rising.

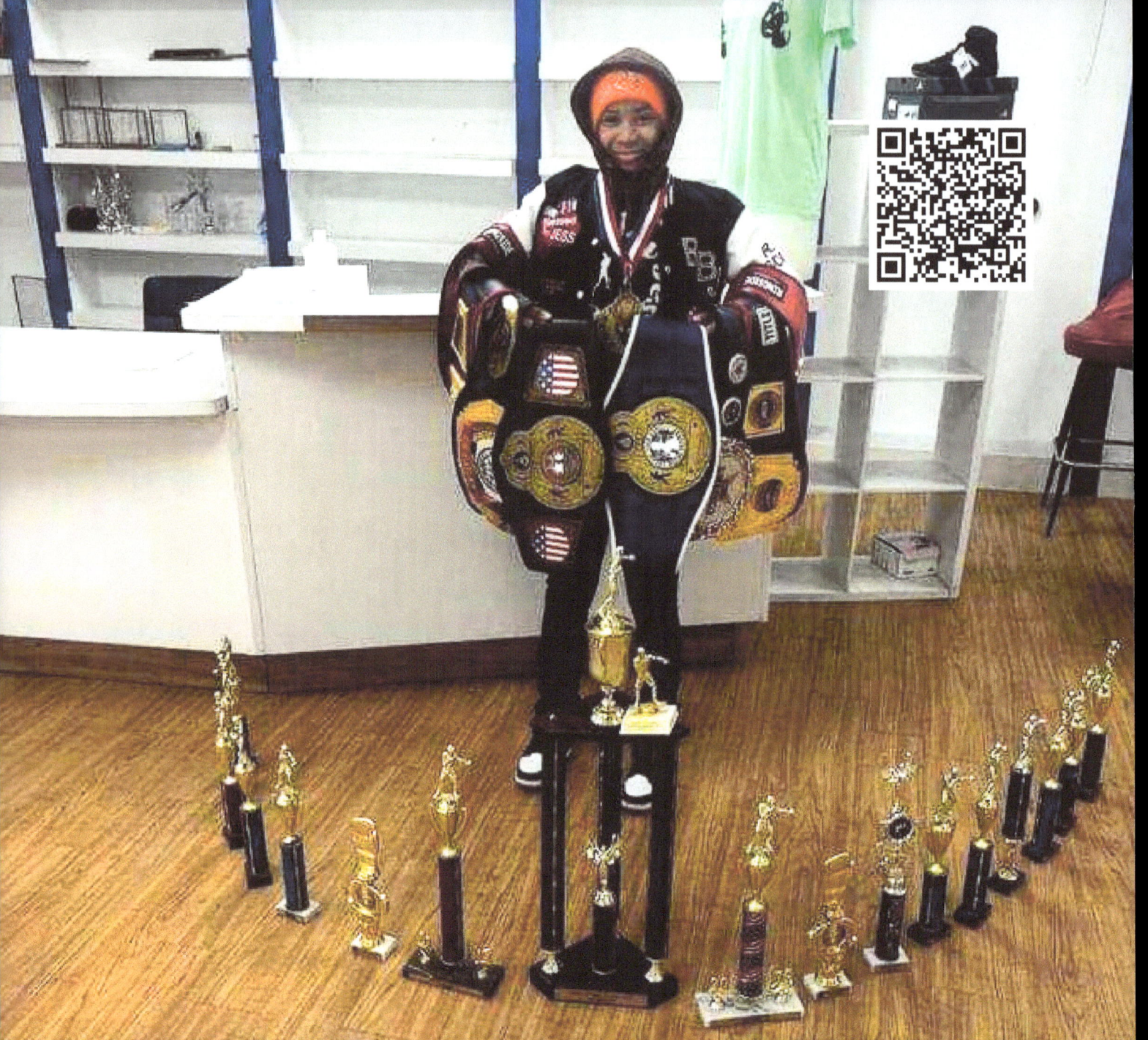

WHO IS
AALIYAH JOHNSON

Aaliyah Johnson of Chicago is primed to conquer the professiona amateur boxing arena, having won six successive fist fights and earning her first Golden Glove belt.

AND THEN IT HIT EM

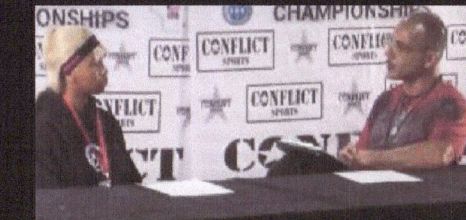
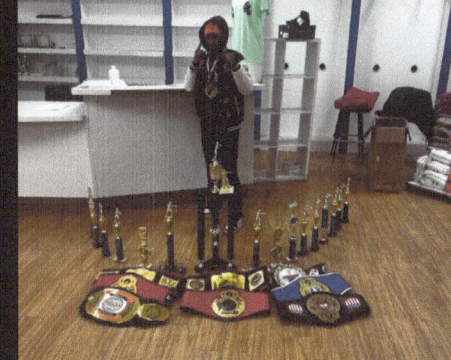
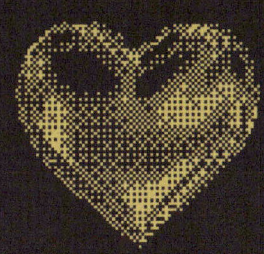
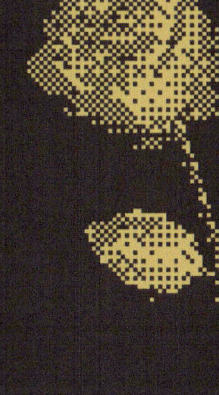
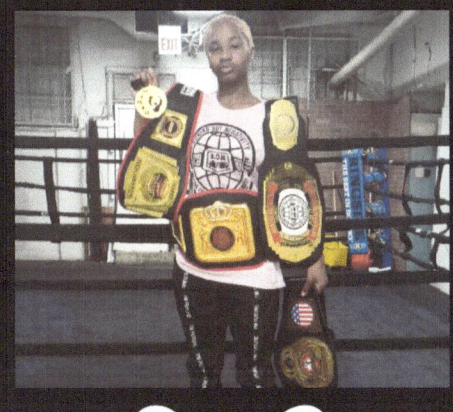

Introducing Aaliyah Johnson, a rising star from Chicago's lively South Side. Johnson has a remarkable record of six consecutive fist victories and has swiftly established herself as a force to be reckoned with in the world of professional amateur boxing. Her path to success has been nothing short of miraculous, characterized by pure persistence and uncompromising dedication to her work.

Johnson was born and bred in Chicago, and his origins are deeply ingrained in the city's vibrant boxing culture. She had a natural ability and desire for the sport from a young age, polishing her skills at local gyms and training facilities. All who observed Johnson's prowess in the ring knew she was destined for greatness.

Johnson won her first Golden Glove Belt, cementing her standing as a rising boxing star. Her unwavering work ethic and brave approach have earned her the respect of fans and teammates alike, cementing her place as one of the sport's most promising young players.

As she rises through the ranks of professional boxing, Aaliyah Johnson serves as an example to aspiring athletes worldwide, demonstrating that with hard work, commitment, and unshakable passion, everything is possible. Keep an eye on this vibrant young boxer as she prepares to make a lasting impression on the world stage.

Unforgettable

By: Kristy Parque

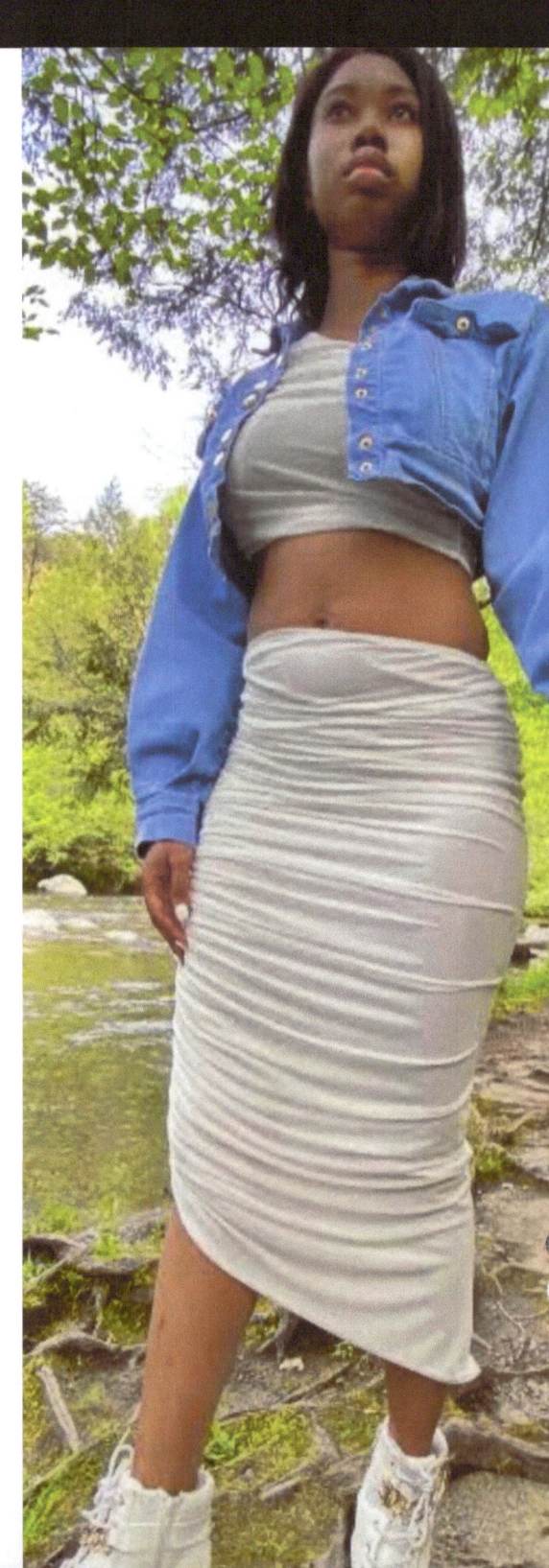

Unforgettable by K. Parque (in honor of my Granny Betty Parque) Live your life to the fullest is the mantra. I'm just trying to be an influence like Frank Sinatra . I have an old soul soul like Nat King Cole .I want to break the mold to adjust how a story is told. You see you're unforgettable. You made me who I am & that's a fact for 21 years. you got me on track. You were a fighter the true definition. of a bounce back. You always focused on what I had instead of what I lacked, & you told me the truth that was that. You inspired me & started a fire in me that made me feel reborn. . You were a pleasant presence in the time of storm. We used to talk 5 times a day the moments never passed away. You taught me to pray about everything. You told me that when I felt that no one was listening to stand tall, lift my voice, & sing. You taught me the value of being life smart not just book smart. You taught me to finish what I start. I'm making you a poem because you were like a melody. You believed in me & gave me my wings. Now I can fly & every time I look to the sky…I see you, I miss you, because you're unforgettable. You're incredible. You're unforgettable too.

What is the poem about? I wrote this poem because my Granny was an amazing lady. My granny passed away a few years ago, but she always taught me the power of being resilient. Resilience is important because it helps to make people tenacious to weather through the storms of life. Some people can impact you and make you feel confident and bring out the best in you. My granny always saw the best in me and supported me and my dreams. She was a woman with an old soul, and she was very wise. She was an educator who believed in the importance of acquiring a good education and pushed me to attend college. When I would get discouraged, she would encourage me, and we spoke several times a day every day until she passed away. She taught me the power of strength, kindness, intelligence and creativity. She believed in my writing and knew that all words are powerful. Granny told me that words are powerful so I must always make sure I'm saying something worth saying. I wrote poetry to show my emotions and to let my inner thoughts be displayed in the most positive fashion

Poems by Kristy Parque

DESCENDANTS OF MARTYRS
BY K.PARQUE

We are sons, we are daughters, we are the descendants of martyrs we are still in slavery cause never departed, our minds are still in chains, but our hearts are not in bondage, we must break free from society's limits on us, but can't nobody stop us but us. The Black Panther Party said power to the people even though we were in a society where we continuously face evil. We were born with societies stain so we must stop and honor the slain and make the world know our names.

We must stand together divided we fall but united we stand tall. We were once so blind. Now we can see clear we hit the glass ceiling, but the sunshine is near, a moment of glory that seems to disappear.

Yeah, I know you cry at night you walk these streets scared. In the end, you will fly high because in life to succeed you will have to fight, in the end you will eventually get it right. Your pain is your story, your life reflects your glory. You were going to give up, but you saw a bright future then you looked up.

No more rainy days or skies full of gray time to stop putting your life on replay fast forward because you will see better days. You dream big but you act hard. You're afraid to tell people who you really are, but you were born to be great, born to be a star, no time to wait your future is not that far.

In the end you'll soar like an eagle; its power in your words is destined for the people. We strain for survival in a world filled with evil; the time is now time to free the people.

Unforgettable by K. Parque
(in Memory of my Granny)

Live your life to the fullest is the mantra.
I'm just trying to be an influence like Frank Sinatra. I have an old soul like Nat King Cole. I want to break the mold to adjust how a story is told.

You see you are unforgettable. You made me who I am & that's a fact for many years you got me on track. You were a fighter, the true definition of a bounce back. You always focused on what I had instead of what I lacked, & you told me the truth that was that.

You inspired me & started a fire in me that made me feel reborn. You were a pleasant presence in the time of storm.
We used to talk 5 times a day, the moments never passed away. You taught me to pray about everything. You told me that when I felt that no one was listening to stand tall, lift my voice, & sing.

You taught me the value of being life smart not just book smart. You taught me to finish what I start. You believed in me & gave me my wings.
Now I can fly & every time I look to the sky...I see you, I miss you, because you are unforgettable.

Dirty Wounds
by K.Parque

Blood falls from the sky instead of rain and it splashes continuously on my windowpane.
It injects like a needle and leaves a stain, God, please come to erase my pain.
The past is not what I gain the future seems like nothing but rain.
Together it won't be such a strain. Our strength and determination are what keep us sane.
Who is to blame? The past continues to baffle my brain, but the future continuously calls my name.
They say clean your wounds, so they don't get infected,
but the truth is they prevent old dreams and nightmares from being resurrected.
Some memories are better if they are not recollected.
These wounds are like puzzle pieces, without the missing piece, it can't be connected.
Dirty wounds that are a signal to wounds that come from deep inside.
You will forever be named strong, with a spirit and soul that will never die.

Why did I write this?

I wrote this poem to talk about the importance of knowing who you are and continuing to fight for what you believe in. I am very open-minded, and it is essential to speak up for yourself and others that are facing injustice. I wrote this power to help people to feel empowered to push on no matter what.

No one is perfect but everyone is a work in progress. It is important to never be silenced despite whatever life throws at you. Know that tomorrow will be better than yesterday, but you must be courageous to see the changes that you desire. Do not be afraid of change.

Where you are from does not have to determine where you are going. Each time period in your life helps you to build you to realize your purpose.

Why did I write this?

I wrote this to help myself to cope with the death of my granny. My granny was one of my best friends and she was supportive of me. She would attend my school events from elementary school to undergrad. She invested in my education as well and was very present in my life.

In life we all may lose someone that is important to us, but we must continue their legacy to honor them with our words and actions. It is important to be able to cope with the loss of a loved one. Sometimes you might not know who to turn to or how to cope but using your gifts and talents can be beneficial.

It is essential to focus on the beautiful memories of your loved one to help you through your grieving period. Use that grief as motivation to excel in everything that you do to make them proud. Appreciate the living and cherish the dead.

Why did I write this?

In life we all go through pain and sometimes it leaves us feeling wounded. We have two choices to give those wounds the time to heal or to let them eat us alive. I use wounds in a literal & symbolic way because sometimes we all have emotional wounds then can turn into physical wounds/ailments. It is important to make sure that we focus on the positive things in life. Do not allow your past pain and experiences to break you. Do not let the dirt(which represents life issues) prevent your emotional wounds from healing.

You are not your past you are stronger because of it. Always know that no matter what you are going through you are not in this world alone. There is someone somewhere out there that loves you.

Going through pain might make you feel wounded and down, but it will not destroy you. Use every life experience as a building block to get through it because you will emerge stronger after the storm.

"POETRY IS LIKE SOUP FOR YOUR SOUL".
- KRISTY PARQUE "LET ME RANT PODCAST"
NEW PODCAST EPISODES WILL BE RELEASED EVERY FRIDAY AT 7PM STARTING NOVEMBER 17TH.
IG:QUEENARI_97
KPARQUE42@GMAIL.COM

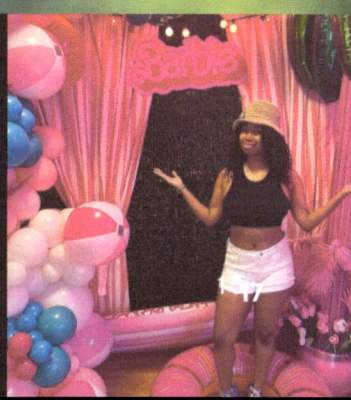

ADVERTISEMENT HERE

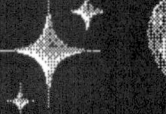 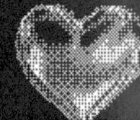 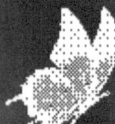

ADVERTISEMENT

SLNP UNSIGNED

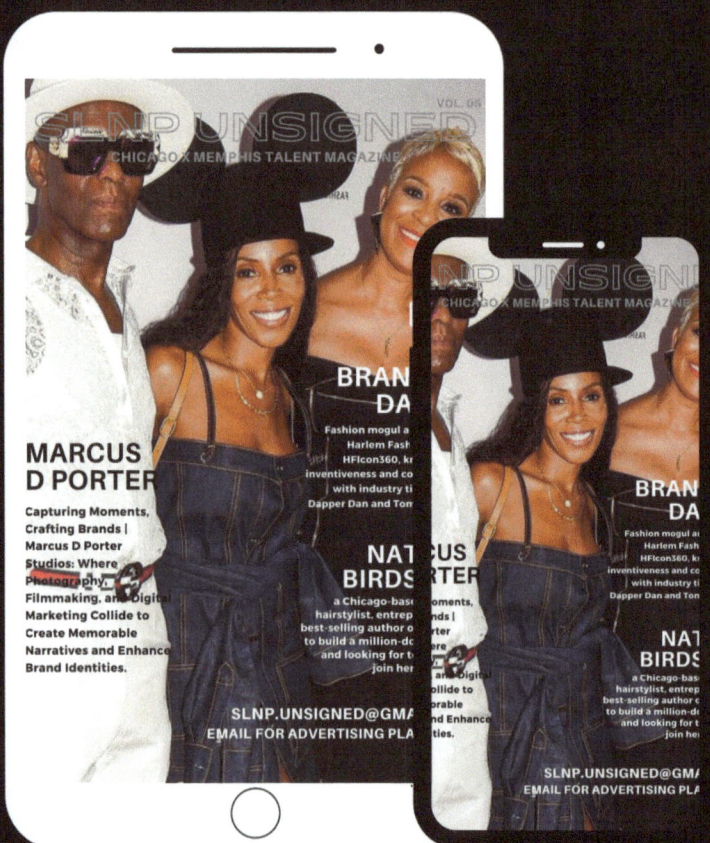

ADVERTISE WITH SLNP UNSIGNED

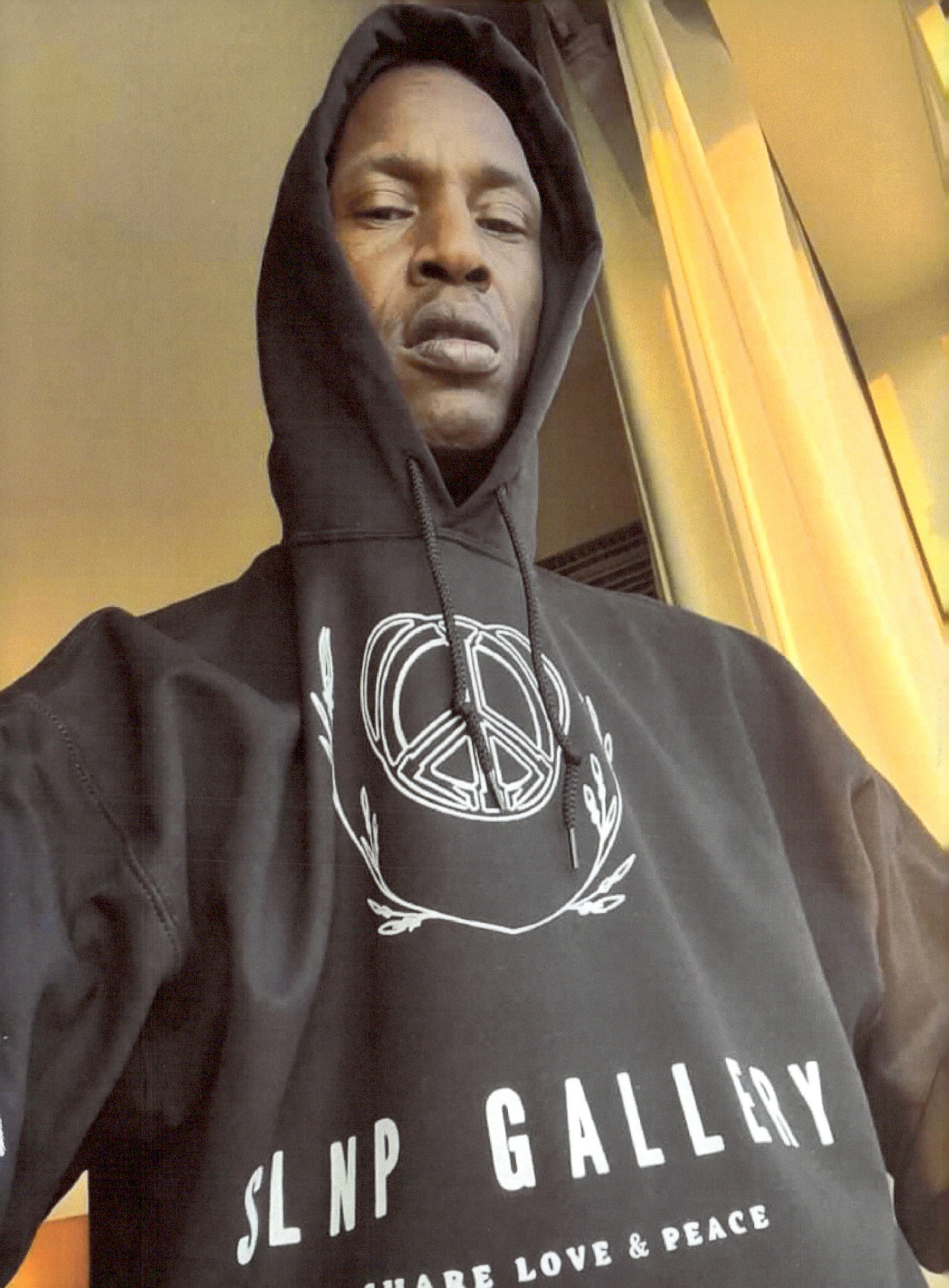

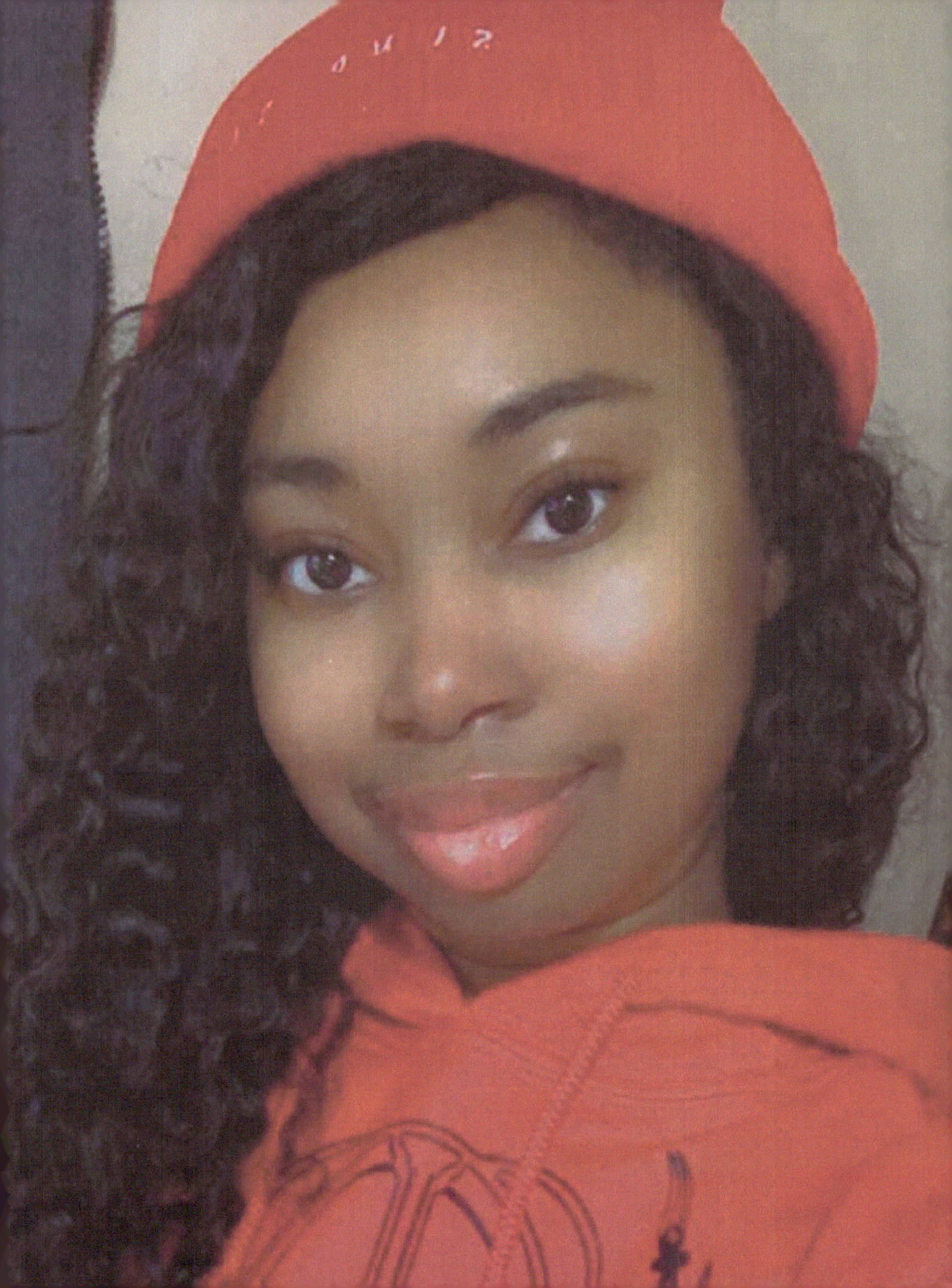

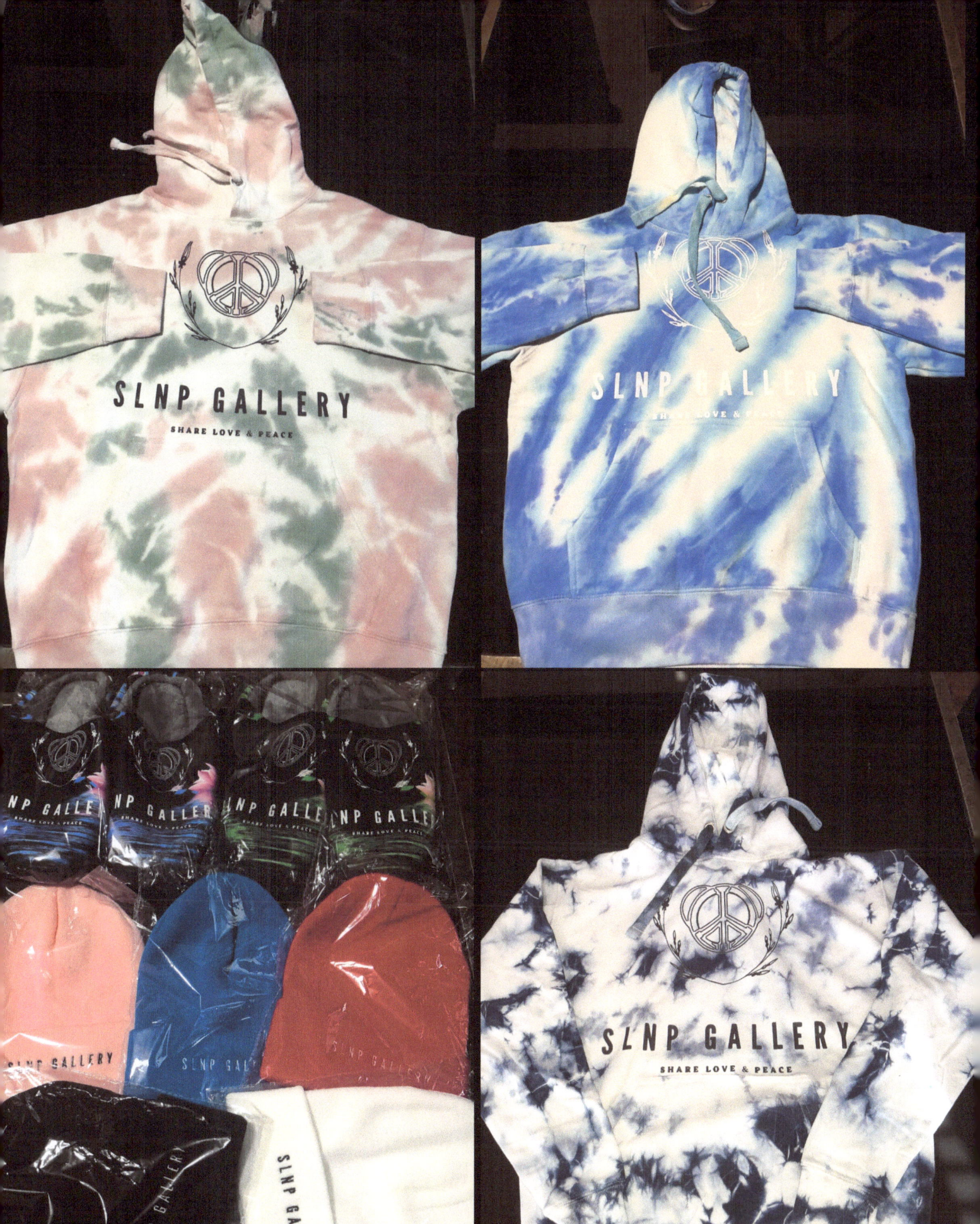

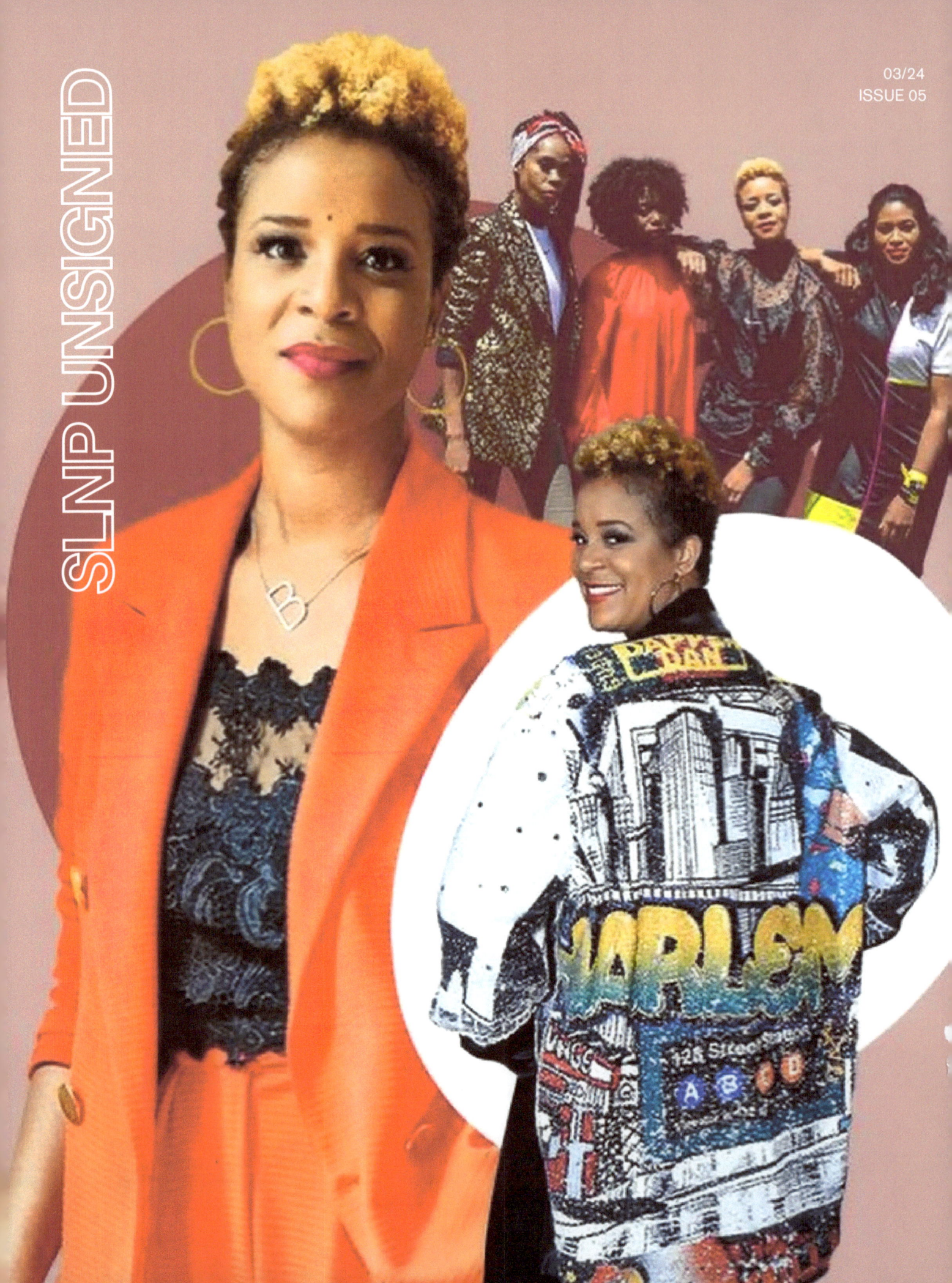

www.ingramcontent.com/pod-product-compliance
Lightning Source LLC
Chambersburg PA
CBHW051838210526
45473CB00005B/1927